D0062522

Racing Along the Razor's Edge

Discourses on Spirituality
by
Swami Ramakrishnananda Puri

Mata Amritanandamayi Center
San Ramon, California, USA

Racing along the Razor's Edge
Discourses on Spirituality
by
Swami Ramakrishnananda Puri

Published by:
Mata Amritanandamayi Center
P.O. Box 613
San Ramon, CA 94583-0613 USA
Ph.: (001) 510-537-9417
Fax: (001) 510-889-8585
Website: www.amma.org
Second Printing March, 2007

Also available at:
Mata Amritanandamayi Mission Trust
Amritapuri P.O., Kollam Dt., Kerala
INDIA 690 525
Phone: 91 476-2897578 / 2896399 / 2896278
Fax: 476-2897678
Email: inform@amritapuri.org
Website: www.amritapuri.org
ISBN   1-879410-94-X

sarva śruti śiroratna
virājita padāmbujaḥ
vedāntāmbuja sūryo yaḥ
tasmai śrī gurave namaḥ

The Guru's lotus feet shine like the gems that are the revelations of the scriptures. The Guru is the Sun that causes the lotus of Vedantic wisdom to bloom. To that Guru, I offer my prostrations.

— *Guru Gita*, Verse 68

Humble offerings at the lotus feet of my beloved Satguru, Mata Amritanandamayi Devi

TABLE OF CONTENTS

PREFACE

uttiṣṭhata jāgrata
prāpya varānnibodhata
ksurasya dhārā niśitā duratyayā
durgaṁ pathastat kavayo vadanti

*Arise! Awaken! Approach the great masters
and become enlightened.
Arduous is the path, as difficult as treading
the sharp edge of a razor. So say the wise.*

— *Katha Upanishad*, Chapter I, Canto 3, Verse 14

This verse from the Hindu scriptures is an apt description of any spiritual path. Though there are millions of seekers all over the world, only a few are known to have attained the ultimate goal. It is very difficult for a person in modern society to cross the ocean of sense pleasures and material desires. Journeying along the spiritual path, with only books to guide us, is extremely difficult. Certain spiritual practices can even be dangerous when undertaken without the guidance of a Perfect Master. But there is no need to be discouraged, for the progress we make along the spiritual path is always of value, regardless of how short a distance we may travel.

Fortunately, God's grace has incarnated on earth in a physical form to carry us across the darkness. Her name is Sri Mata Amritanandamayi Devi, but she is known all over the world simply as Amma or Mother. She teaches us the technique of walking along the razor's edge (the spiritual path) without cutting ourselves or falling off. With the help and loving guidance of a supreme, compassionate master like Amma, we can even race along the spiritual path.

Some basics of the delicate art of balancing spirituality and worldly life are given in this volume. There is something in this book for everyone. Whether it appeals to the advanced seeker or to one who is new to the spiritual path is up to the individual. This book is mainly addressed to those who want to experience inner peace and joy while living fully in society.

May you enjoy this book and be blessed with an intense longing for the inner presence of the eternal Mother.

Swami Ramakrishnananda Puri
Amritapuri, 27 September, 2003

SRI MATA AMRITANANDAMAYI DEVI: AN INTRODUCTION

"An unbroken stream of Love flows from Me toward all beings in the cosmos. That is My inborn nature."

— Amma

In the state of Kerala in Southern India, nestled on a peninsula between the Arabian Sea and the Kayamkulam backwaters, stands the Amritapuri Ashram. Amritapuri has been sanctified by the presence of Sri Mata Amritananda-mayi Devi, Divine Mother and revered Satguru to millions all over the world.

To the people of this age, bereft of a living faith and with hearts thirsting for pure love, Amma has come as a torrential shower of divine love. Ever established in the unbroken experience of supreme truth, She accepts every-one as Her own Self. Taking suffering humanity upon Her lap, soothing our pain and giving us hope, She dispels the darkness from our hearts and leads us on the path toward perfection and everlasting joy.

Through almost three decades of tireless service, Amma has personally counseled and consoled millions of people from all walks of life and from every corner of the globe. Amma wipes each one's tears with Her own hands and removes the burden of their sorrows. The compassion, tenderness and deep concern that She shows to everyone, the spiritual charisma, innocence and charm that come so naturally to Her, are all unmistakably unique.

An embodiment of all that She teaches, Amma devotes every moment of Her life to lifting the burden of suffering humanity. Through the medium of devotional songs, through simple talks replete with vivid illustrations and strikingly lively examples, and through the example of Her own incomparable life, Amma is conquering the hearts of people everywhere.

A BRIEF LIFE SKETCH

On the morning of the 27th of September 1953, in the village of Alappad on the west coast of Kerala, a baby girl was born. Her parents gave Her the name Sudhamani. She came into this world not in tears as babies usually do, but with a beaming smile on Her face, as if prophesying the joy and bliss She was to bring to the world. From Her earliest childhood She was fully aware of Her true nature but, like the playful Krishna, preferred to act as a mischievous child. She would later surprise Her parents by recalling every minute incident that took place during the first few months of Her life.

Though born divine, Sudhamani spent the years of Her childhood and teens immersed in intense spiritual practices in order to present a living example for the world. Even as a small child, She could often be found absorbed in deep meditation, totally oblivious of Her surroundings. By the age of five, She had already begun composing devotional songs addressed to Lord Krishna, songs brimming with poignant longing and often laden with deep mystical insight. Forgetting Herself in Her love for the Lord, She would pour Her heart and soul into these melodies. Her sweet voice became a source of great joy to the villagers.

When Sudhamani was nine, Her mother became ill, and the entire workload of cooking and housekeeping fell upon Sudhamani's shoulders, forcing Her to leave school. Sudhamani did Her grueling work without a hint of complaint, joyfully offering every moment of Her long hours of hard labor as prayers to the Lord. She willingly accepted every obstacle, every bit of ill treatment She received from Her family, and found Her only solace and support in the constant remembrance of Her beloved Lord Krishna. When Her workday ended at midnight, instead of going to sleep Sudhamani would spend a good portion of the rest of the night meditating, singing and praying to the Lord.

Another quality that was clearly manifest in Sudhamani from this tender age was Her love and compassion toward Her fellow human beings. As part of Her household duties, Sudhamani often visited neighborhood homes to collect food for Her family's cows. There She patiently listened to many tales of woe, especially from the elderly, who often told Her how they were being neglected and ill treated by their grown-up children and grandchildren. Through their stories, Sudhamani observed that the same people who as children had prayed for the health and longevity of their parents now cursed their parents when they grew old and infirm. She saw that worldly love always has an underlying selfish motive. Though only a child, Sudhamani did whatever She could to ease the suffering of Her elderly neighbors. She washed their clothes, bathed them and even brought them food and clothing from Her own home. This habit of giving away things from Her family's house often landed Sudhamani in great trouble. However, no amount of punishment could stop the expression of Her inborn compassion. Sudhamani would say to Her parents, "The very purpose of My taking this body is to suffer for the ignorance of others."

As Sudhamani reached Her teens, Her love for the Lord grew to indescribable proportions. Her ecstatic moods became more and more frequent; She danced and sang in bliss, intoxicated with God and totally oblivious of the world. In Sudhamani's eyes, the whole Universe was pervaded by Krishna alone. It was not long before Sudhamani entered into a profound mystical union with Her Lord, a union so complete that She could no longer distinguish between Krishna and herself.

One day She had a glorious vision of the Divine Mother of the Universe. This experience was followed by a continuous state of God-intoxication. Day and night Sudhamani was overwhelmed with yearning for union with the Divine Mother. Her family members and many of the villagers were at a complete loss to understand Sudhamani's sublime moods and began to harass Her in every possible way. She was finally forced to leave Her home and spend Her days and nights out in the open. The sky became Her roof, the earth Her bed, the moon Her lamp and the ocean breeze Her fan.

When Sudhamani's own family and the villagers rejected Her, it was the birds and animals that kept Her company and became Her loyal friends. The animals brought Her food and lovingly rendered Her whatever service they could.

Sudhamani immersed Herself for months on end in the most rigorous and austere spiritual practices. Her entire being was ablaze with love and yearning for the Goddess. She kissed the earth and embraced the trees, perceiving the Divine Mother within them all. She wept at the wind's touch, feeling it to be the Divine Mother's caress. She was often found immersed in samadhi for hours or even days on end, displaying no sign of external awareness. Her spiritual practices culminated in the total dissolution of Her personal self into the Divine Mother of the Universe. In Her song, "Ananda Veethi," Amma portrays this experience as follows:

"Smiling, the Divine Mother became a mass of effulgence and merged in Me. My mind blossomed and was bathed in the many-hued light of Divinity... Thenceforth, I saw nothing as apart from My own Self..."

She realized that "the entire Universe exists as a tiny bubble within My Self." The all-pervasive primordial sound "Aum" spontaneously sprang forth from within Her being. Sudhamani now experienced that all forms of God are manifestations of the one Atman.

Later, when asked about Her poignant devotional songs and the need for the intense austerities She had undergone during Her earlier years, Amma replied, "Did not Rama and Krishna worship Lord Shiva and Devi, though they themselves were Avatars? Nobody who is born with full consciousness declares from childhood that, "I am Brahman," for this would imply that the other person is not Brahman. When one has realized the Absolute Unity, to whom can one speak and about what? That state is beyond all words and descriptions. If you wish to communicate with someone who is deaf and dumb, you cannot speak to him or her in your own language—to get the message across, you have to communicate in sign language. Though you are using sign language, it doesn't mean that you yourself are deaf or dumb. Likewise, Avatars may undergo severe austerities, or you may see them meditating, but that doesn't mean that they really need to do so. They do it only to set an example for the world."

The Amritapuri Ashram

After this initial period of intense austerities, Amma dedicated Herself fully to Her mission of serving the poor and suffering and spreading the message of spirituality. She began receiving large numbers of people who flocked to Her for blessings, and the home where She was born was transformed into an ashram. Many young disciples soon began to gather around Her, and She started training them in accordance with the sannyas tradition of India. The monastic name, "Mata Amritanandamayi," was conferred upon Her, though She continued to be known popularly as Amma. The once tiny ashram has now evolved into the headquarters of Her international mission. Thousands of devotees pour into the ashram each day for Her *darshan*, and over two thousand spiritual aspirants reside there permanently, engaging in spiritual practices and selfless service under Amma's direct guidance.

WORLD TOURS

Amma has been traveling to many different countries regularly since 1987. Spreading the message of love and spirituality, She has led thousands of spiritual programs around the globe. Every year She visits about twenty nations. In the West, the media often describes Amma as the "Hugging Saint." Amma's programs are given extensive coverage by TV and print media in every country She visits.

In 1993 at the Parliament of World's Religions Centennial in Chicago, Amma was elected as one of three presidents of the Hindu faith. That same year, *Hinduism Today*, an international journal on Indian culture, conferred the Hindu Renaissance Award on Amma. In 1995, Amma was invited to speak at the Interfaith Celebrations in New York to commemorate the 50th anniversary of the United Nations. In 2000, Amma delivered a major presentation to the Millennium World Peace Summit in the UN General Assembly Hall on the topic, "The Role of Religions in

Conflict Resolution." In a landmark address on the condition and capabilities of women, "The Awakening of Universal Motherhood," Amma spoke to the Global Peace Initiative of Women Religious and Spiritual Leaders at the United Nations Assembly Hall in Geneva in October 2002. On this occasion, She was presented with the prestigious Gandhi-King Award for Non-violence. Previous recipients of this award include former President of South Africa Nelson Mandela, UN Secretary General Kofi Annan, and renowned primatologist and UN Messenger for Peace, Dr. Jane Goodall.

AMMA'S DARSHAN

The Sanskrit term *darshan* means "vision" and is used to describe the meeting with a holy person, especially a Self-realized Master. Amma's darshan is unique. As the embodiment of supreme motherhood, She welcomes every person who comes to Her, listens to his or her problems, offers advice and guidance, and brings reassurance to the grief-stricken. On special occasions, Amma manifests Her identification with Devi (the Divine Mother), and the darshan is called Devi Bhava. Earlier, Amma used to give darshan in Krishna Bhava as well.

About the meaning and significance of bhava darshan, Amma says, "All the deities of the Hindu pantheon, who represent the numberless aspects of the One Supreme Being, exist within us. One who is established in the Divine can manifest any of them by His or Her mere will for the good of the world. Krishna Bhava is the manifestation of the Pure Being aspect, and Devi Bhava is the manifestation of the Eternal Feminine, the Creatrix, the active principle of the Impersonal Absolute. However, it should be remembered that all names and forms are mere mental projections. Why should a lawyer wear a black coat or a policeman a uniform and a cap? All these are merely external aids meant to create a certain feeling or impression. In a similar manner, Amma dons the garb of Devi in order to strengthen the devotional attitude of the people coming for darshan. Amma's intention is to help the people reach the Truth. The Atman or Self that is in Me is also in you. If you can realize the Indivisible Principle that is ever shining in you, you will become That."

CHAPTER 1

THE CAUSE OF ALL SORROWS

THE FUNDAMENTAL PROBLEM

L ife, for many people, is a constant struggle to find solutions to innumerable problems that cause suffering. According to the Hindu scriptures, ignorance about one's own Self is the cause of all sorrows. We are the Supreme Consciousness, but we take ourselves to be a complex of the body, mind and intellect. In truth, whatever happens to the body, mind, and intellect, the eternal Consciousness which enlivens it is not at all affected. In the *Bhagavad Gita*, the eternal Consciousness, *Atman*, or Self is described as

> nai'naṁ chindanti śastrāṇi nai'naṁ dahati pāvakaḥ
> na cai'naṁ kledayanty āpo na śoṣayati mārutaḥ
> acchedyo 'yam adāhyo 'yam akledyo 'śoṣya eva ca
> nityaḥ sarvagataḥ sthāṇuḥ acalo 'yaṁ sanātanaḥ
>
> *Weapons do not cut it, fire does not burn it,*
> *water does not wet it, and wind does not dry it.*
> *This (Self) is eternal, all-pervading, stable,*
> *immovable, and primordial.*

> — *Bhagavad Gita*, Chapter II, Verses 23 - 24

We focus on meeting the needs of this complex because of our mistaken identification with the body and mind. This identification creates a lot of desires in us. We could not possibly fulfill all our desires, but this longing is ever present. These unmet desires often cause sorrow.

We also generate expectations of the way our life is going to unfold. Unfortunately, the outcome does not always match our anticipated result. We may expect that we will marry a specific person, that we will be successful at work or that our child will be in an honors program at school. When our expectations go unmet, we experience unhappiness.

Attachment also plays a role in sorrow. For example, when we value the accumulation of money and material objects too much, we become attached to these items, and grief is certain to follow when our car is stolen, our investment sours, or we suffer some other material loss.

Negative qualities such as selfishness, lust, anger, greed and jealousy affect our decisions and actions, thereby increasing the likelihood of anguish and misery.

If that isn't enough cause for sorrow, indiscriminate decisions and the resulting wrong actions (mental, verbal, and physical) can produce negative karma which ultimately results in suffering either in this life or in the next.

Thus, we are the ones who create sorrow for ourselves. God does not create suffering. Actually, God creates a beautiful world. It is our mind that makes it otherwise. Amma tells a story in this regard.

Two men were sitting in a garden near a rose bush. Looking at the fully blossomed roses, one man started thinking, "Such beautiful roses! If I give one of them to my girlfriend, she will be so happy. Such a beautiful smile will blossom on her face." Immersed in such thoughts, the man sat there looking intently at the rose bush, forgetting all else.

The other man sitting there, however, became disturbed looking at the very same roses. He was thinking to himself, "I gave so many flowers like these ones to my girlfriend. In spite of all that, she betrayed me and went off with another man. I can never forgive her for this." With such bitter thoughts in mind, he even became angry at the flowers and stomped on them, crushing them under his feet. Then, hoping to find some peace of mind, he went off in search of a liquor shop.

The mind, alone, is the cause of our bondage and lack of freedom. We must discipline the mind in order to find peace, joy and freedom.

Moving from sorrow to joy is difficult to accomplish through our own effort, but a *Satguru* (True Master) can help us overcome the negativities that cause sorrow.

DESIRES

We all have desires, but they may or may not be fulfilled. In answer to the question, "Why are all our wishes not satisfied?" Amma says, "If everything were to happen as we wanted, then the harmony in creation would be lost."

Doctors want more patients, but none of us wants to get sick. If lawyers wish to have more clients, then more crimes, accidents, and fights must occur. However, we all want peace and unity in society. Liquor shop owners want more and more people to drink so that they will have increased business, but parents don't want their children to drink.

No one wants to die; some people even want their dead body cryogenically frozen so that in the future when science learns to bring the dead back to life, such people will be able to resume their life. But still, coffin makers pray for more business.

If all wishes were to be fulfilled, there would be no order on the planet, only chaos and disharmony. In fact, it is only because some desires are not fulfilled that at least some harmony exists in the world.

It must also be pointed out that all the happiness we get from external objects is nothing more than borrowed happiness—happiness does not belong to the objects themselves. Actually, the happiness we think we derive from these objects is only a reflection of the happiness within us. That is why children are generally happy with trivial objects.

EXPECTATIONS

Expectations can cause sorrow for several reasons. If our expectations are not fulfilled, it leads to disappointment. In some people, disappointment generally leads to anger. In others, it will lead to frustration or depression.

Even if our expectations are fulfilled, they can still lead to suffering. If one expectation is fulfilled, our desires grow and we anticipate that other expectations will also be fulfilled. In this way, our greed and desires grow and gain strength. The amount of suffering we experience is commensurate with the strength of our desires and expectations.

This doesn't mean that we should not have any expectations, but we have to be able to remain unaffected when our expectations are not fulfilled.

An action can bring about various types of results. For example, suppose we are afflicted with a disease. We may take medicine for it. Instead of simply believing that the medicine will restore our health, we should be fully prepared for any one of the following results:

1) The disease may be cured completely.

2) The disease may be partially cured.

3) The disease may not be cured at all.

4) We may develop an allergy, complication, or side effect from taking the medicine.

In other words, the result of an action can be:

1) as we expected.

2) more than what we expected.

3) less than what we expected.

4) no result at all.

5) something entirely different from what we expected.

If we expect, we must expect all the above possibilities. We have to be prepared to face any of these results. Assimilation of this concept is real maturity. It is immature not to be prepared to accept whatever might occur.

We are all mature in some ways. We have to become mentally and emotionally mature as well. Amma says that our bodies are growing wider and taller, but our minds are not growing. We need to put forth effort to cultivate this mental and emotional maturity.

NEGATIVE QUALITIES

We all exhibit negative qualities from time to time. Qualities such as impatience, greed, jealousy, anger, stubbornness, resentment, anxiety and arrogance surface no matter how hard we try to behave lovingly. These qualities cause great harm to our sense of well-being and to our relationships. Once the mind becomes agitated due to these negative qualities, clarity in decision-making is often compromised.

There are generally four types of people:

1) Those in whom there is a great deal of agitation and negativity but who are not aware of it—such a person believes that there is nothing wrong with him or her. As the saying goes, "Ignorance is bliss."

2) Those who know that they have negativity within, but don't see any reason or need to remove it. Even though they may learn to live with it, they will continue to suffer, experiencing anger, resentment, and many other negative qualities. These emotions are a problem for them as well as for those around them.

3) Those who know that there is a lot of negativity in their minds and who want to remove it. They don't want to live with these problems; they want to enjoy peace of mind, calmness and quietude. So, they try to remove their negativity. It is only this group that tries to take up spiritual practices like meditation, prayers and scriptural studies or who approaches a Master.

4) These are the exceptionally few—the *Mahatmas*[1], like Amma, who have completely transcended all the negative qualities of the mind. In fact they have no egocentric mind—their mind is one with the Universal Mind. For them, there are no problems.

We all know that it is harmful to ourselves and to others when we experience anger, resentment, or anxiety. Intellectually, we know it's destructive, but we don't have the strength of mind or the training to overcome these negative qualities.

---

[1] A *Mahatma* is a God-realized (Self-realized) person, but he or she may or may not be interested in guiding others along the spiritual path the way a Satguru does. All Satgurus are Mahatmas, but not all Mahatmas choose to be Satgurus.

All the spiritual practices we do are to train our mind to overcome our negativities. Unfortunately, most of us are not training our mind; our mind has trained us, and our negative qualities have taken control.

Even when we are in Amma's powerful presence, we often find that something or the other is disturbing us. I have heard devotees say to Amma, "Amma, to be in your presence is the best opportunity for meditation, but even in your presence I am not always able to meditate properly."

LACK OF AWARENESS ABOUT THE CHANGING WORLD

Suppose you receive a telephone call. As soon as you pick up the receiver and listen to the first words of the caller, you find out who is on the other end. If it is your partner or spouse, you may say something like, "Hello darling, how are you? I miss you so much!" But if it's your boss at the other end, you won't say the same thing. If you did, you might even be fired from your job!

It is the same case with different objects and situations in the world. In order to relate appropriately, we have to know the nature of the objects, people and situations we are dealing with.

To complicate matters, attitudes, objects and situations are always changing. Today we may have a very nice car or computer, but tomorrow it may be fit only for the junkyard. Similarly, people don't sustain a consistent attitude.

Today a person may be our best friend; tomorrow he may turn out to be our worst enemy.

SEEKING HAPPINESS IN THE WRONG PLACES

Nobody says, "I want to be happy only in the morning; I don't mind being unhappy in the evening." Nor does anyone say, "I want to be happy only when I am at work; I don't want to be happy when I am at home," or "I want to be happy only when I am driving my car." In other words, we want happiness that is unlimited and unconditioned, irrespective of time, place or objects. Nevertheless, we always search for happiness in people, objects, and circumstances, which are changing and impermanent by their very nature. It is totally illogical to expect unchanging and permanent happiness from anything that is changing.

It is not that objects can't give us happiness. They can give us happiness, but the happiness that we get from them is incidental and not intrinsic. An object can make a person happy at a particular time or in a particular situation but never always and forever. If we buy ourselves a brand new Mercedes Benz, we will probably feel happy about it. Whenever we drive the car or even think about it, we might feel happy. On the other hand, if a close relative or someone we love dies, we'll feel very sad. In that situation, no matter how many times we may think about or drive our Mercedes, it won't make us happy. This is because the happiness that we derived from the car was incidental and not intrinsic. If the happiness we got from the car had been intrinsic, it would have made us happy at all times. In fact, if we depend on such objects for our happiness and support, we will be disappointed.

Amma says that we should all be like a bird sitting on a dry twig. A bird sitting on a thin, dry twig knows that even a gentle breeze is enough to break its fragile perch. So the bird will always be alert and cautious, ready to fly away at any time.

When we lose the objects of our interest or desire or when they leave us, without feeling sad, we must be able to proceed toward our goal just as the bird on the twig flies away the moment the branch breaks.

Objects have only a limited capacity to make us happy, but they have an unlimited capacity to make us unhappy. Try not to give undue importance or value to objects and not to expect too much from anyone.

Amma says that seeking unchanging happiness from changing objects is like expecting cold water from a desert. We must not allow our mind to be dependent on objects or people for peace and happiness because they are not under our control. Instead, we should learn to adjust our minds according to the situation. This is what Amma means when She says we should learn to air-condition our minds. Amma tells a story to illustrate this point.

One day a king wanted to walk around his capital city. As he was walking along the road, he stubbed his toe against a small stone that was sticking out of the ground, and his toe started bleeding. He got angry with his servants and guards and shouted, "How could you let this happen to me?!" He commanded that the next day, before he went for a walk in the evening, all the roads in the city were to be carpeted. The ministers scratched their heads because they didn't know how to accomplish this task. They were wondering where they could find such long carpets. Among them was an old and wise minister who was rather bold. He said to the king, "Your Majesty, instead of spreading carpets all over the roads, would it not be wiser for you to wear a pair of good shoes?"

Similarly, instead of trying to adjust everything for our convenience, we should try to adjust ourselves to the external conditions. This is possible through understanding spiritual principles and performing spiritual practices. If we can gain spiritual strength, it will serve us like a shock absorber for a vehicle. The shock absorber helps the vehicle sustain the jolts and bumps on uneven and rough roads. Likewise, our lives are full of ups and downs, and it is this spiritual strength that helps us to absorb the setbacks in our lives.

ATTACHING INAPPROPRIATE VALUE

If we make poor decisions without proper discrimination as to what has real value, sorrow will be the result. Many students commit suicide when they do not pass or do not make the expected grade in their examinations. Sometimes, during a volatile sporting match, fans will fight each other over an umpire's call. A larger perspective would indicate a response more in keeping with the relative importance and value of these situations.

Sometimes we do give the correct value to things. For example, suppose we have a brand new pair of expensive shoes. Even though they are very expensive, we don't keep them in our briefcase or in our closet. We wear them on our feet and walk even on dirty roads without any fuss. They are just shoes and were purchased to be worn. Unfortunately, we are not able to extend this discriminatory approach to all situations in life.

I would like to narrate an incident which highlights how Amma gives only appropriate value to each and every object in the world. In the early days of the ashram, we often didn't have enough food to eat. We didn't even have enough good clothes to wear. Whenever we held programs outside the ashram, the *brahmacharis* (celibate disciples) would share the few good clothes available. Also, in those days, Amma was very particular that whoever came to the ashram should be fed, and only after everybody had been given food were the brahmacharis allowed to eat. On many days there would be no food left for us. On those occasions Amma would go to the neighboring houses to ask for alms.

One day a poor woman from the neighborhood came to Amma saying that her daughter's marriage had been arranged. As she was very poor, she needed Amma's help. Even though the ashram was struggling financially, Amma assured her that She would help. I was sitting next to Amma when She called one of the residents and asked him to fetch something from Her room. He brought a box and handed it to Amma. She opened it and inside was a new, expensive gold chain, perhaps a recent donation from a devotee. I was wondering what Amma was going to do.

Without any hesitation, Amma handed the expensive gold chain to the woman. She was very happy and profusely thanked Amma. I felt quite agitated because we ourselves were struggling so much financially. How could Amma do this? Before I could say anything, the woman had left. I couldn't control my shock. I asked Amma, "How could you do that?"

I gave Amma a long lecture. "Do you know how expensive that chain is?" I was working in a bank at the time, so I knew the market value of gold. I told Her, "I could have taken it to the bank for you and gotten a good amount of money for it. I do not think what you did was correct."

"Is that so?" replied Amma. "Why didn't you tell me this earlier? Bring that woman back at once! Hurry up!"

I felt very proud of myself to have had the clarity of vision to correct even Amma's mistake. In those days I had no idea of Amma's greatness as a Self-realized Master. My spiritual understanding was miserably poor. Just like many pseudo-intellectuals, I also thought that I had more knowledge and experience in the ways of the world. I was convinced that Amma wanted to retrieve the chain from the woman, so I went and brought her back. She was wondering what was going on. Amma said to her, pointing at me, "This brahmachari says that it is a very expensive chain." I was so impatient that I wanted to say to the woman, "So give it back to us." Amma felt my impatience and told me to keep quiet. Amma continued, "Because the necklace is so expensive, don't pawn it or sell it for a cheaper price than it's worth. Make sure you get a good price for it."

I suddenly felt very ashamed of having been so ignorant of Amma's compassion.

This is just one example of how Amma doesn't give undue importance or value to the things of the world. It doesn't mean that material wealth is not important, but we have to realize its limitation. Material wealth is not everything. If so, all the rich people would be happy and joyful. I have seen many rich families crying to Amma for various reasons. Spiritual wealth is far more important. By spiritual wealth, I mean spiritual strength and maturity born out of the understanding of the ephemeral nature of the world and its objects. Spiritual wealth enables us to smile even when we come face to face with death.

Soon after people started flocking to see Amma, there were those who were violently opposed to the bhava darshans. There were even several attempts on Her life, including one by Her cousin who thought that Amma's behavior was going to somehow spoil the family name. When he threatened Her with a large knife, Amma was not at all perturbed. Amma simply laughed and replied, "I am not at all afraid of death. The body must meet its end sooner or later, but it is impossible for you to kill the Self. Now that you are determined to put an end to My physical existence, let Me meditate for a while, and then you may kill Me while I am in meditation." Through Her under-standing of the nature of Her true Self and of the world, Amma was able to calmly confront even a threat to Her life; She was not even angry or upset with Her attacker.

THE LAW OF KARMA

Scientists have recently begun to confirm that this is not our only birth. It is not yet possible to prove beyond any doubt, with existing scientific and technological development, the truth of rebirth and past births. But it is only reasonable to ask: if every action has an equal and opposite reaction, what is the action that causes a child to be born with deformity, or in a poor family, or as a prod-igy? He or she has not done anything to deserve it in this birth. It is logical to conclude that there must have been a prior lifetime in which that person "earned" this result. In some families one child is very intelligent whereas the other is not. What is the reason for this? The child must have done something in a previous birth to deserve it. The children born to the same parents have so many other marked differences. And there are tyrants like Hitler and Stalin who have massacred millions of people. When and how are they going to experience the result of such cruel acts? Definitely, they will have to suffer through many lives to come.

According to the law of karma, every action has its invariable effect on the doer. There is no escape from the chain of karma as long as one has the ego. Also, the results of one's actions are not limited to that person alone. It also affects other members of the society. If we do something good, not only are we, but the world at large is affected positively. If we do something selfish or harmful, that, too, will have its effect on others. Suppose we have the habit of drinking too much liquor. Then, while intoxicated and driving our car, we hit a person who may be trying to cross the road very carefully. That will result in our going to court and the other person going to a hospital. It will have other consequences to the families of both parties. Thus, one wrong or careless action of a single person may adversely affect the lives of many.

That is why Amma says that we are not isolated islands but connected to each other like the links of a chain. Whether we know it or not, the actions we perform always have an effect on others.

Two hardened criminals were exiled to a remote, desolate island. Many years passed. One day they were sitting on the beach crying uncontrollably, thinking about their fate. Suddenly, a bottle was washed ashore. One of them picked up the bottle and opened it. Immediately a genie came out. It was so happy to be released from the bottle that it offered one boon to each of them in return for their help. The first one said to the genie, "I have been suffering on this island for so many years, separated from my dear children and family. I want to be with my family." Instantly the first criminal was back with his family in a far-away land. When he was gone, the second criminal was all the more sad because of being alone. He told the genie,

"I never had a family or friend in my life. He was my only friend who really loved me. I miss him so much. All that I want is that my friend be brought back here." In no time, the first one came back to the island and the genie disappeared.

Karma, both our own and that of others, is an important factor in determining whether or not we will succeed in a particular effort. To avoid unnecessary suffering, it is important for us to understand the role karma plays in our lives.

I had appeared for my graduate examination and was expecting to pass it with good marks. When the results came, I was surprised to find that I had failed in one paper. I was shocked, for I had done that paper very well. I applied to the university for re-evaluation of that paper. When the results came, I was declared as having passed in first class. Later inquiries revealed that the professor who originally evaluated my paper was going through a difficult phase in his life. It seemed that he had had a quarrel with his wife, and his wife had eloped with the neighbor who was a truck driver. The professor was very much upset over this matter. Whenever he would hear the noise of a truck, he would become extremely restless and agitated, sometimes hysterical, because it would remind him of the truck driver with whom his wife ran away. Many trucks went by his house, making him more and more restless. Because of this, he was not able to give proper attention to his academic duty of evaluating the papers properly. Thus, his karma had an adverse effect on my life also.

papers properly. Thus, his karma had an adverse effect on my life also.

These examples show us that there are many factors that can intervene between our effort and its results. We may pray to God to fulfill a desire, but whether it is fulfilled depends upon so many things: the intensity and sincerity of our prayers; the effort we put forth; our past karma, and sometimes others' karma as well. Many of these factors our beyond our control. If the factors that are not under our control are to become favorable, we need God's grace. Our effort alone cannot bring about the desired result.

THE NATURE OF SUFFERING AND SORROW

Every person born on earth has his or her share of sorrows and joys. Out of the karma which is accumulated from the past, whatever one is destined to experience, good or bad, in the present lifetime is called *prarabdha*.

Our prarabdha can be of different types:

1) Prarabdhas that can be fully overcome by performing positive actions. These are like a benign or harmless cancer that can be removed once and for all through a simple surgery.

2) Prarabdhas that can be reduced or partially removed by our efforts. This type of prarabdha is like the malignant cancer which can be removed but which has a chance of returning.

3) Prarabdhas that don't have any remedial measures. We will have to go through them. Amma gives the example of terminal cancer. This type of prarabdha cannot be avoided. One has to suffer it.

One may wonder what Great Masters like Amma teach the world with the example they set by their lives. They show the world how to face difficult situations with inner maturity. They inspire us to follow their example. Many of us may have faced excruciating pain and sorrow in life. When we hear how Jesus forgave His enemies at the time of His crucifixion, we can also gain the courage to face any situation without a feeling of hatred, without resenting anybody.

Amma underwent many troubles in Her early life in spite of Her tremendous devotion and love for God. She was not disappointed that God gave Her such a hard life. Amma viewed Her hardships as opportunities to learn that behind the love of human beings there are always some selfish interests. If these interests are not met, worldly love immediately turns to hate. Only God loves us unconditionally, without any expectation. Amma understood this and started loving the very people who brought only sorrows and troubles to Her. Unfortunately, it is very difficult for us to forgive our enemies, much less love them. If we are able to do this, we are transforming our hearts into the abode of God.

By Her response to such hardships, Amma showed how even in the midst of such difficult circumstances one can stay focused on God and face the challenges courageously.

Amma was not sad or upset that Her parents did not give Her love and affection. She thought, "Why should I seek love from anyone? Instead, let me give love to everyone."

Amma doesn't expect anything from anybody. Amma does Her duty without being concerned about the result. That is real spirituality.

EGO

According to the Hindu scriptures, the first product of our ignorance about the nature of our true Self is the ego. In Sanskrit the ego is called *ahamkara*. Ahamkara can also be translated as "the sense of an existence separate from the rest of the universe." All our desires, expectations, attachments, negative qualities, and even our karma arise from the ego.

Ego is the feeling of "I," i.e. "I am doing," "I am enjoying," or "I am suffering." When we wake up, what is the first thought that enters our minds? It is "I." All other thoughts follow from this first thought.

This feeling of "I" gives rise to all our problems. When we are identified with the ego, we will have desires, expectations, and attachments related to establishing the safety, security and comfort of the ego. When these desires, expectations and attachments are frustrated, or when our ego is injured, we react with anger, hatred, fear, depression, etc. Amma says it is the ego and the negative qualities arising from it that block God's grace from reaching us.

We may feel that we have transcended the ego by doing so many spiritual practices and performing so much *seva* (selfless service). We may even think, "Look how much more seva I perform than that person. I am so much more selfless than he is."

It is important to remember that the ego is very subtle and clever. There is a story in the great epic *Mahabharata* (the book describing the Mahabharata War) that shows how even advanced spiritual seekers and great devotees can fall into the trap of the ego.

After the battle was over, Arjuna, with Lord Krishna as his charioteer, and the righteous Pandavas returned to their camp. As soon as the chariot reached the camp, Krishna halted the chariot and said, "Arjuna, please get down."

Arjuna thought to himself, "I fought and won the battle. Krishna was only my charioteer. Actually, he should get down first." Thinking thus, he asked Krishna to get down first. Krishna refused, telling Arjuna that he really must get down first. Even though Krishna had already revealed His divine form to Arjuna on the battlefield, imparted the entire *Bhagavad Gita* to him, and saved him from certain death during the war, Arjuna still would not listen to Krishna and wanted Krishna to get down before he did.

In spite of experiencing Krishna's divinity on so many occasions, Arjuna's ego tricked him into thinking he was greater than God. However, as Krishna was obstinate on the point, Arjuna got down from the chariot before the Lord. Krishna calmly waited for Arjuna to walk some distance away before getting down Himself. The moment

He did, the chariot burst into flames. So many powerful weapons had been used against the chariot during the day's battle. It was only because of Krishna's presence that the chariot had remained intact and Arjuna had been able to win the battle. Arjuna fell at Krishna's feet, finally realizing that it had been with the Lord's power alone that he had fought and won the battle.

In truth, no matter what we may do, we cannot remove the ego by ourselves. Amma says that ego is the only thing in creation that was not created by God. The ego is our creation, and we cannot undo our own creation. For that, we need the help of a Satguru. Removing the ego is the Satguru's primary job.

CHAPTER 2

CHAINS OF CONDITIONING

UNDERSTANDING CONDITIONING

W e are always looking for the right job, right boss, right spouse, right friend, and so on. We forget that we also have to be the right person. Men want a chaste wife like Sita (the holy consort of Lord Rama), but they forget that they have to be virtuous and righteous like Lord Rama.

There is hardly any perfect person (other than the Mahatmas and Satgurus) or perfect job or perfect spouse. When we look for perfection, we either lose a good opportunity or get disappointed. Looking for perfect things, we sometimes exchange one problem for another.

We hope that by changing the situation or the person, we are going to solve the problem. This thinking is the result of past habits and conditioning. If changing external factors worked for us in the past, we assume this strategy will continue to work. We may have more potential capacity for changing ourselves for the better, but we limit ourselves based on prior conditioning.

Amma gave the following example of conditioning in Her speech during the Global Peace Initiative of Women Religious and Spiritual Leaders in Geneva. When an elephant is a baby, it is accustomed to roaming freely in the forest. After being captured, it is tied with a sturdy chain to a strong tree or pole. It will keep tugging and pulling on the chain, but to no avail.

After some time the baby elephant realizes that all the tugging and pulling will not help. Therefore, it stops pulling and stands quietly. Now it is conditioned. When the baby elephant becomes a mature elephant, it can be tied with a thin rope to a frail post or tree.

The adult elephant could easily snap the rope and freely walk away, but it does not go anywhere because it is conditioned to think that it is not possible to break the chain. Likewise we are constantly being conditioned, consciously or unconsciously, by our surroundings, our parents, our friends, the movies and TV programs we watch, etc.

There was a retired military officer who was disliked by the children in the neighborhood because of his short temper. One day they wanted to play a trick on him. As he was walking home from the market with a basket of eggs in his hand, one of the boys shouted, "Atten-tion!" As soon as the military officer heard the word "attention," he dropped the basket of eggs from his hands and stood at attention without moving. This was due to his previous conditioning.

Amma says that in order to fully enjoy life, freedom from the conditioning of the past is absolutely necessary. In fact, there are many choices available to us in any difficult situation in life. When we are faced with a critical situation, our ability to make the right decision is inhibited.

Our conditioning from the past hinders our capacity to make good use of the choices available to us.

Because of our conditioning, we tend to react in a certain way or according to a particular pattern. Most of the time, we are not conscious of what we are doing or what we are saying. Thus, instead of consciously responding to the situations in life, we come up with mechanical reactions. When somebody praises us, we become happy and might even say, "He or she is such a nice person." When somebody criticizes us, we become defensive. When somebody insults us or gets angry with us, we may get upset or angry in return.

DEVELOPING POSITIVE CONDITIONING

Positive conditioning helps us manifest good qualities spontaneously. Let us take the example of chanting a mantra.

Initially, we do not know anything about a mantra. We are not even aware of our ignorance about the mantra. Then we come to know that there is something called a "mantra." From a Guru[2] we can learn what a mantra is, receive mantra initiation, and understand the method of chanting and practicing. In the beginning stages we will forget to chant the mantra regularly as we are not used to

---

[2] Master. In this book, *Guru* is used interchangeably with *Satguru*, or True Master.

chanting a mantra. So we have to make a conscious or deliberate effort to chant the mantra.

After chanting the mantra regularly for a long period, it becomes as natural as our breathing. We don't have to even think that we have to chant the mantra; it goes on continuously without any effort or deliberate thinking on our part, no matter where we are or what we might be doing. It has become an automatic process. This is how we cultivate a habit or discipline in our life.

For most of us, qualities like anger, impatience and jealousy occur spontaneously without any effort. Instead, we need to learn to manifest admirable qualities like love, compassion, patience, kindness, etc. We need a continuous and regular effort and practice to do this. In a Master like Amma, these positive qualities manifest spontaneously.

Many of Amma's devotees are already spontaneously exhibiting some good behaviors, like saying the mantra, "Om Namah Shivaya" while greeting other devotees. Some devotees greet even their office colleagues and other friends saying, "Om Namah Shivaya."

Devotees can be seen prostrating before sitting in front of Amma. This habit has become so natural that they prostrate before they sit even when Amma is not in the hall or when they sit to eat, talk, or read, etc.

Mahatmas are well known for spontaneously manifesting all the divine qualities. Many years ago, I saw Amma demonstrate this divine spontaneity in a remarkable way. Toward the end of Devi Bhava, Dattan, a leper with ruptured skin all over his body and blood and pus oozing from many of his wounds, entered the temple. As soon as I saw him, a sudden feeling of aversion and fear of infection came over me. My instantaneous reaction was to get up and run out of the temple. Amma's spontaneous response was to get up from Her seat and rush toward Dattan to hug him. She did not wait to think whether She should wear gloves or a mask before hugging him. Such was the spontaneous expression of Her divine qualities.

CHAPTER 3

BREAKING THE CHAINS
OF CONDITIONING

LEARNING FROM ADVERSITIES

If we overcome our negative conditioning, adversities can strengthen us. When Amma experienced hard times at the hands of Her parents, the villagers, and Her relatives, She did not break down. Instead, She made use of these adversities to understand the nature of the world and the shallowness of worldly love. Her parents and relatives saw Her behavior and Her constant praising of the Lord as eccentric, and they behaved accordingly. Even though She was kind to everyone, She rarely received a kind word or praise from anyone. Amma, instead of seeking love and affection from anybody, directed Her heart and soul to God. She learned not to expect anything from anybody. She went on doing Her duty and let God take care of the rest. Because of Her clear understanding of the selfish and egoistic nature of human beings, Amma's love for others did not diminish due to the hardships She suffered at their hands.

Amma knows that today's friend may become an enemy tomorrow and an enemy may turn out to be a friend. Hence, Amma's love and compassion for those who praise Her and those who criticize Her remains the same.

In fact, many people who created trouble for the ashram and for Amma during the initial years are now the beneficiaries of Amma's various charitable projects. Many such people are today helping Amma carry out Her service activities.

It is said that experience is the best teacher. However long we stay in the presence of a Guru, unless we learn from our experiences, we cannot make spiritual progress. Amma gives the example of a swimming teacher. While we are learning to swim, at some point our teacher will let go and force us to swim on our own. This is to instill confidence and courage in us so that we will learn to swim by ourselves. Similarly, at times, God or the Guru may give us trials and tribulations so that we will develop our own skills and strength and learn to make good choices.

Failure to make the right decision or the right choice not only deprives us of the best opportunities in life but also creates negative emotions, which in due course build up a lot of stress and tension. I would like to illustrate this point with a small incident from my early days with Amma. It was during the time when Amma used to appear in Krishna Bhava followed by Devi Bhava. One group of brahmacharis would sing during Krishna Bhava and the other group during Devi Bhava.

Two of us had just learned to play the *tabla* (a type of drum often used in Indian music). During this initial stage of learning the tabla, we were both eager to play the drums as much as we could, and we would take turns playing for Amma.

In those days, there were only a few brahmacharis, and Amma would often call one or two of us and give us an opportunity to meditate sitting next to Her during Devi Bhava. One day during Devi Bhava, it was my turn to play the tabla. Before playing, I went for darshan thinking of returning immediately to play the drums. However, when I went for darshan, Amma asked me to sit by Her side and meditate. I was in a dilemma. I was intent on playing the tabla, and yet here was an opportunity to sit and meditate near Amma. I didn't want to disobey Her, so I sat there.

As I started meditating, the *bhajan* (devotional singing) also started, and the brahmachari who had already had his chance started playing tabla again. I was so upset and disturbed! I got very angry with him. How dare he take my turn? But I could not get up and confront him, since Amma had asked me to sit next to Her.

Instead of meditating, I was having a real fight with the other brahmachari in my mind. Almost half an hour passed. Though my eyes were closed, I wasn't meditating. Suddenly, I felt someone tapping on my head like playing the tabla. I opened my eyes, and it was Amma. Amma asked me what I was doing. Before I could answer Her question, She asked me to go play the tabla. She knew that I was thinking only about the tabla and getting annoyed with the other brahmachari. There is no better atmosphere for meditation than sitting next to Amma in Devi Bhava, but because of my negative emotions, I wasted the opportunity.

If Amma had faced the same situation, things would have been entirely different. Amma would have made a different choice. She would have concentrated on meditating rather than worrying about playing the tabla or getting angry with someone.

There is always something to learn from any experience in our life, whether it is a pleasant experience or an unpleasant one. That is the advantage of having a human birth endowed with the innate human qualities of intelligence and discrimination. If we look at Amma's life, we see that whenever there was some sad or seemingly unfortunate incident, Amma not only learned a lesson from it, She saw it as an opportunity to move closer to God.

Even during the pre-ashram days Amma was well known for Her hard work. From four in the morning She would work non-stop until 11 at night or even midnight. In addition to the heavy load of work in Her house, on many days Amma would be sent to Her relatives' houses to help them with their household chores as well. Some of these houses were far away from Amma's house. For a short period Her parents gave Her money to travel by boat along the backwaters. She enjoyed boat travel very much. She would chant "Om" along with the sound of the engine. Looking at the ripples on the surface of the water, She would totally forget Herself. Every moment of Her life was used to connect with God.

Later, Amma's parents decided that they would not give Her money. They told Amma, "You must walk. We can no longer pay for the boat." Amma did not feel upset.

She said, "Fine, then I will go on foot." She had to walk eight or 10 kilometers, but She enjoyed the walk even more than the boat ride. It would take Her at least three times the time it had taken to travel by boat. Amma was happy because She could be alone for such a long time. She was able to walk in solitude by the beach or along the backwaters, and She was able to chant more mantras and more prayers. Thus She used this apparently negative situation in Her life to Her advantage.

There are many such situations happening in our lives, and if we really employ our discrimination we can use them to our advantage. It is not possible for us to dictate which experiences we should have or not have; this is beyond our control. Our wisdom or capacity lies in converting any situation to our advantage.

A woman was having a lot of problems both at work and at home. Whenever something would go wrong at work, she would immediately remove a photo from her bag and look at it intently for some time. After regaining her composure, she would peacefully resume her work. Having observed this for a few days, one of her colleagues asked her, "Who is in that photo? How can it give you so much strength and calmness? Is it your spiritual teacher or your favorite movie star or a baseball player?"

"No, no. It is my husband's photo," replied the woman.

"Oh! That is really wonderful. I did not know you had so much love for your husband," replied the colleague.

"I don't," said the woman. "It's just that every time a problem comes and I start to lose my composure, I only have to look at his photo, and all other problems seem insignificant. Compared to him, any problem is manageable." In short, this woman was able to keep things in perspective and derive strength from an adverse situation.

TAMING THE WILD ELEPHANT

In the early days when we first came to Amma, we didn't know how one is supposed to behave with a Guru or how to respect the Guru. Only after we began studying the scriptures did we start to understand the greatness of the Guru and the code of conduct required of us in our relationship with the Guru. Before that we had no way of knowing about the greatness of the Guru because Amma never told us.

She never said, "You should respect me," or "You should prostrate to me," or "You should behave in such and such a way in front of me." Even though we needed to hear it, She would not say it. Sometimes we disobeyed Her and behaved disrespectfully toward Her. We would even express a bit of our anger toward Her. But Amma, out of Her compassion and understanding, would accept us with all our negativities. Even if we made a mistake or disobeyed Her, She would simply smile or keep quiet. She wouldn't try to enforce discipline on us. Later, when we realized our mistakes, we'd go and apologize to Her.

One day Amma said something that I didn't want to accept, and I started arguing. When someone argued with Amma or disobeyed Her, She usually didn't object. On that particular day, however, Amma started arguing with me, which took me by surprise. She said, "No, what you said was not correct." But I was in no mood to relent. Toward the end I was shouting at the top of my voice. Then suddenly Amma got up and went to Her room. I didn't want to stop the argument because I wanted to make sure that I'd won. So I got up and followed Amma. She went to Her room and closed the door, but it didn't close completely. She sat down and started meditating. I couldn't continue my argument. I waited outside, thinking that Amma would come out of Her room shortly and I could continue from where I'd left off. I waited for fifteen minutes, but nothing happened. 45 minutes later, Amma still hadn't come out. She was still meditating. I didn't have the patience to wait any longer. I also didn't want to disturb Amma while She was meditating, so I thought I'd continue later.

Only after two and a half hours did Amma come out of Her room. By that time I was involved with some work and had to go to a nearby town. Still, I kept thinking that what I had said to Amma was correct and that I would prove it. Even though my mind was full of anger and arrogance, I couldn't help feeling surprised that even after such a strong argument Amma could meditate as though nothing had happened.

Slowly and steadily love with its infinite patience won over my anger, and my mind cooled down. It was nearly two weeks before I had a chance to be with Amma again. I apologized for the way I had behaved and said, "Amma, after that heated argument you went to your room and became immersed in meditation. I, on the other hand, struggled for 10 days to be able to meditate. As soon as I closed my eyes, the only thing I could think of was how to defeat you in that argument. I was meditating on this for 10 days! I couldn't even chant one mantra peacefully. How was it possible for you to meditate immediately after that fight as though nothing had happened?"

Amma replied, "As soon as I knew it was a waste of time to argue with a useless fellow like you, my mind became introverted. A split second was enough for me to go within."

As for me, even after 10 days, I hadn't realized that my meditation was being disturbed by my own negativity. Sometimes it takes many years to realize this, sometimes many lifetimes. A Master will make us realize it in a short time.

Amma says that anger is like a knife without a handle; it injures both the person who is attacked and the attacker. We know very well the ill effects of anger on our body and mind as well as on our family and society at large. Anger unleashes many destructive hormones in our body. The whole body burns as if on fire, and it wreaks havoc in our immune system. What we may not know, however, is how anger can add to our chain of karma and block God's grace from reaching us. When the ego is hurt, our immediate reaction is to get angry. Out of anger we perform many indiscriminate words and actions. Through such words and actions, we may even hurt an innocent person. Amma says that when we get angry with an innocent person, that person may even cry out to God, "Oh God, I haven't done anything wrong. Why am I being treated in this way?" The vibrations of these painful feelings will definitely reach us, darkening our aura just as soot darkens a glass. In the same way that sunlight will not penetrate glass blackened by smoke, these impressions will block God's grace from reaching us. Amma also says that when we get angry, we lose energy through every pore in our body. In this way, a lot of hard-earned spiritual energy is unnecessarily dissipated.

Suppose we are in the habit of getting angry with people. When the opportunity arises, let us try not to get angry. By cultivating awareness and patience, we can slowly overcome anger.

In trying to transcend anger, first train the mind to recognize the negative aspects of anger. Then watch anger as it manifests in various situations. Just by watching it, as a separate and distinct observer, we are loosening its hold on us. As long as we are identified with our emotions like anger, lust and fear, we will never be able to bring them under our control. We need to create a space between the emotions of our mind and ourselves.

Just as we tame a wild elephant or a new horse, we can first try to tame the expressions of anger in our words and actions. Later we can watch it as it originates in the mind and remain as a witness to the rise and fall of anger within us. We are watching anger, just as a person on the beach watches the rise and fall of waves in an ocean. Finally we will become totally free from its damaging influences.

CHANGING EMOTIONS, CHANGELESS LOVE

Often, Amma displays human emotions just to make us feel close to Her. One moment Amma may shed tears listening to a devotee's problem. The next moment Amma will be laughing, sharing in the joy of another devotee. Suppose Amma is in tears while listening to one devotee's woes. The next devotee coming for darshan tells Amma, "Today is my birthday." If Amma continues to shed tears, how would the devotee whose birthday it is feel? So as each person comes up for darshan, Amma acts like a mirror, reflecting the state of his or her mind. Amma may express anger toward somebody for his or her mistakes, but the next moment, She can hug the same person, whereas it can take days for us to hug a person with whom we are really angry. Amma can erase and replace the emotions in Her mind as and when She wants to. She has the pencil to write something in Her mind and the eraser to remove it.

We may think when Amma is angry or upset, that She doesn't like us. That is not true. She simply says what needs to be said for our own spiritual growth and moves on. She does not hold on to Her anger at all. Amma's emotions are just like a line drawn on water. How long will a line drawn on water last? However, I wish to make it clear that just because Amma is not attached to Her emotions, it doesn't mean that She doesn't love us or care about us.

As soon as you've had your darshan, Amma is ready to receive the emotions of the next person. Amma's love is like the ocean, and all the emotions She expresses are only waves, foam and froth. Essentially these are all water but in different form and shape. Similarly, underlying Amma's every action and word is pure love. It is possible for us to attain that state, too, but it requires tremendous practice, alertness and awareness.

If we are overpowered by our own emotions, we can't help a single person—we can't even help ourselves. When we are able to transcend our emotions and our negativity, then we can help many others.

CHAPTER 4

AMMA'S LOVE

THE PURPOSE OF AMMA'S LIFE

When Amma was very young, She used to go to the neighboring houses to collect scraps of leftover food (mainly tapioca peel) for Her family's cows. She found that at many of the houses, the children did not have enough to eat. The children would sleep in a fetal position because of their hunger. In other houses, She found that the elders were totally neglected by their children. Many people were sick without money for proper treatment.

When Amma saw these miseries, She became very angry with Nature. As revenge for all the suffering in the world, She wanted to burn Herself to death inch by inch.

Then a voice from within told Her that if people are suffering, it is because of their fate which is the result of their past actions. The voice continued, "The purpose of Your birth is not to give up Your body like this. There are millions of people who need Your help and guidance. Your life is to serve them. Through serving them You are serving Me (the Ultimate Truth)."

Amma acknowledged, "If it is their fate to suffer, it is My duty to help them."

GOD'S LOVE IN A HUMAN BODY

"She stands here in front of us,
God's love in a human body."

— Dr. Jane Goodall, presenting Amma with the 2002
Gandhi-King Award for Non-violence

Many years ago, soon after I joined the ashram, one of the ashram residents was caught stealing. We informed Amma, but She didn't take any action. After a few months the same person was caught stealing again, and once again, Amma ignored the matter. Some of us got angry about this and wanted to discuss the issue with Amma.

I was extremely upset about the prospect of this boy staying in the ashram any longer. I knew that if I were to talk to Amma about this boy, Amma would defend him out of Her love and compassion, and then I might argue with Amma because I would not be able to agree with Her. So I wrote a letter to Amma, telling Her that if She did not send the boy away from the ashram, I might have to leave the ashram.

Having read the letter, Amma called me and said, "You may be a good person. You may know what is right and what is wrong, and you may go to some other ashram and do your spiritual practices if you wish, but this poor boy doesn't know what is right and wrong. If I do not give him enough love, the right guidance, and correct him lovingly, who else is going to help him? He might even land in jail. I am going to keep him here even if all of you leave the ashram."

When the boy who was caught stealing heard this, tears rolled down his cheeks. From that moment he was transformed and never stole again.

Amma's divine love and compassion strengthens and nourishes us and gives clarity to our mind as we relax in Her presence. Many are able to overcome their addictions, attachments, worries and problems through the strength of this love. True love rejects nobody. It accepts everyone. Amma says, "For Me to reject someone would be like rejecting My own Self because I am not separate from anyone and no one is separate from Me." So Amma can only love everyone. She can never hate anyone.

Just as light and heat are the nature of the sun, love and compassion are the nature of all Great Masters. How we make use of this love is up to us. The nature of the river is to flow. We can drink the river water, wash ourselves in it, sit on the riverbank and enjoy the cool breeze or even spit into the river. The river doesn't mind. It just goes on flowing. Likewise, Amma just goes on giving and giving.

It is said that in the presence of a person who is established in supreme love, even animals that are hostile and ferocious to other creatures and beings relinquish their hostility and remain calm.

Many years ago, one of the dogs that used to be with Amma became mad. It ran out of the ashram and bit several people. When people started chasing it to kill it, it somehow entered the ashram. Its mouth was frothing as happens with a mad dog. People were shouting, "It's a mad dog, kill it, kill it!" A few people started to run away to a safe distance.

I shouted, "Don't run, don't run, there is no need to worry! Amma will take care." But being afraid for my own safety, I was among the people who were running! I continued to run as far away as I could.

Hearing the commotion, Amma came out of Her hut. In a moment She realized what was happening. She walked toward the dog calling him, "Mon, mon!" which means, "My son, My son!"

Some of us were shouting to Amma, "Please go away, Amma. The dog is mad. It will bite you." Amma took no notice of our warnings. Amma kept walking toward the dog. Contrary to our expectations, the dog stood still as though mesmerized, and Amma started stroking the dog. She asked for some food to be brought from the kitchen. The person bringing the food was afraid to go near the dog. He brought the food and held it out to Amma from a distance. Amma took the food and fed the dog with Her own hands and then ate the balance of the food which was drenched with the saliva of the dog.

All of us were terrified as we watched what Amma did. We were afraid that Amma would become infected with rabies. Amma ignored our warnings and concerns. We all insisted that She should get a rabies shot, but She would not and She did not. Amazingly, nothing happened to Amma although the dog died in a matter of minutes, clearly proving that it was rabid.

I was totally overwhelmed by what I saw. I was very curious as to why Amma ate the dog's leftovers. When I asked Her about it, Her response brought tears to my eyes. She said that by eating the balance of the dog's food, She was ending the remaining karma of the dog once and for all—taking it on Herself. Thus, the dog's soul was liberated from future births. The mad dog had been able to feel Amma's love and stood quietly.

Even our so-called friends and relatives cannot love us as Amma does. Amma explains, "If we do 100 good things and one bad thing, people will discard us. But Amma will accept you even if you do 100 bad things and nothing good at all."

To illustrate the limited love of our kith and kin, there is a story of two backpackers who are very close friends. As they are hiking, they see a huge bear that is about to attack them. One backpacker quickly opens his pack and takes out a pair of running shoes. He starts to take off his boots and change his shoes when his companion says, "Hey, you are never going to outrun the bear. What's the use of wearing running shoes?" The backpacker with the running shoes replies, "Who says I have to outrun the bear? I just have to outrun you."

This is an example of worldly love. When our life is in danger, we no longer care for our near and dear ones. None of us will be ready to exchange our life for the life of a dying friend.

That is why Amma says, "Don't expect anything from the world and people in the world because selfless love is very rare." Expectation leads to disappointment and frustration. Expecting unchanging and pure love from a changing and selfish world is foolish.

FRIENDLINESS

adveṣṭā sarva bhūtānāṁ maitraḥ karuṇa eva ca
nirmamo nirahaṁkāraḥ samaduḥkhasukhaḥ kṣamī

Friendly and compassionate to all and
without any touch of hatred;
devoid of possessiveness and arrogance;
ever content and contemplative;
alike in happiness and misery;
dear to Me is a person with such qualities.

— *Bhagavad Gita*, Chapter XII, Verse 13

One day a new devotee approached Amma with a problem. She said to Amma, "Amma, you always say to love everyone. Unfortunately, I am not able to do so. I am not able to love anyone with a full heart. What can I do?"

Amma softly replied, "Daughter, don't worry if you are not able to love all; at least try not to harbor hatred toward anyone. That will slowly lead you to the state of loving one and all."

The devotee later exclaimed, "I was asking this question to many people and even some psychologists. Nobody could give me a satisfactory and practical answer. When

Amma gave me Her reply, immediately my heart was relieved of a great burden."

Maitri or friendliness toward all beings is an important characteristic of a true devotee. We have already seen that a real devotee does not harbor hatred toward any being in the world. Through the word maitri, Lord Krishna makes it clear that the hallmark of a true devotee is not only the absence of hatred, but also a positive and vibrant feeling of friendliness and fraternity toward all beings, for such a devotee truly sees the Lord in all creation.

The *Srimad Bhagavatam*[3] says that he who worships the Lord only in the form of the Lord's image is a primitive devotee. A genuine devotee worships and serves the Lord seeing Him in the entire creation. The friendly disposition of a devotee toward all beings springs from true love. It is spontaneous and comes naturally to him.

On the other hand, the friendliness that we commonly see in the world is influenced by likes and dislikes and is usually limited by considerations of caste, creed, wealth, status in society, etc. It is mostly based on selfishness and mutual interests. Thoughts of personal gain are the motivating factor behind worldly friendliness. Even though most businesspeople may show friendliness and behave lovingly toward their customers, it is only an external

---

[3] The *Srimad Bhagavatam* describes in detail the lives of the 10 incarnations of Lord Vishnu, especially Krishna and his childhood sporting. It upholds the supremacy of devotion. *Srimad* means "auspicious".

show. They behave in this way keeping an eye on the profits they will receive from their customers. Once they think that there is not much benefit to be gained by showing friendliness to a particular customer, their enthusiasm slackens and all the friendliness fades away.

I recollect a story which reveals the nature of the type of friendliness we usually see in the world today. Once a young boy was given a basketful of tomatoes by his mother, who asked him to sell them in the marketplace. He was also told the price at which he should sell them. As he was selling the tomatoes, his friends would come to buy from him, and he would offer them a special discount. In the evening the boy returned home, having made a good profit. His mother, who had come to know of the special discount that her son had offered to his friends, asked him, "How did you still manage to make such a good profit?"

The boy replied, "I give them tomatoes at a price less than the normal price because they are my friends, and I, in turn, take some tomatoes off the weighing balance because I am their friend."

The friendliness a devotee feels for others is universal and untainted by any selfish considerations. In one of his poems, the Great Master Adi Sankaracharya[4] elaborates this as follows: "Shiva and Parvati are my parents, all the devotees of the Lord my kinsmen, and the three worlds my

---

[4] Adi Sankaracharya was a Mahatma who re-established the supremacy of the *Advaita* philosophy of non-duality at a time when Sanatana Dharma was on the decline.

native land." Tulsidas, well known for his rendering of the *Ramayana* in Hindi, has also said, "There are no high and low castes among devotees. A devotee of the Lord is indeed a Brahmin, even if he is born in a low caste." There was a deep friendship between the great king Lord Rama and the boatman, Guha. Lord Krishna, born to a royal family, and Sudama, a poor Brahmin, were close friends as well. These examples show us that the friendliness of great souls cuts across narrow divisions.

A true devotee of the Lord, by his or her mere presence, spreads vibrations of love and friendliness all around. Such friendliness is not limited to human beings but embraces the entire creation.

One of the ashrams established by Adi Sankaracharya is in South India in a place called Sringeri, by the side of the river Tunga. There is a legend behind this ashram. Once Adi Sankaracharya reached Sringeri during his travels across the length and breadth of the country. Walking along the bank of the river Tunga, he was suddenly taken aback by an unusual sight.

A cobra was using its outstretched hood to shield a pregnant frog from the scorching heat of the sun. Adi Sankaracharya immediately sat down in meditation in order to understand the cause behind this surprising scene. He realized that once upon a time a great sage had been living in that place. The sage loved all beings, and he loved wild animals, serpents and birds as his own children. Because of the influence of his hallowed presence, the enmity between animals that were natural enemies disappeared and was replaced by a feeling of love and friendliness. The greatness of the *rishi* (sage) was such that, centuries later, this friendliness continued to prevail.

How true indeed are the aphorisms of the sage Patanjali:

> ahimsā pratiṣṭhāyām tat
> saññidhau vairatyāgaḥ
>
> *In the presence of the One who is established in Ahimsa (non-violence), all enmity vanishes.*

Amma's life is a shining illustration of such universal maitri. An embodiment of universal motherhood, She is perfectly loving to everyone—rich or poor, young or old, sick or healthy—irrespective of any distinctions whatsoever. Amma's love is so spontaneous and natural that everyone feels that Amma is his or her very own. No one is a stranger to Her. Even the worst of sinners and the most stonehearted of people are moved by the all-consuming love and friendliness of Amma.

A few years ago, a festival was being celebrated in a famous temple in Kerala. Suddenly, a fight broke out between two groups of people, and the whole temple premises became like a battlefield. A curfew was imposed. Police had to come and disperse the crowds using force. In that process, many people were injured.

There was one senior police officer who was very rough and tough, and he beat many people mercilessly. On a later occasion, he was on security duty during the inauguration of the Amrita Institute of Medical Sciences and

Research Center, Amma's hospital in Kochi, Kerala. As the Prime Minister of India, the Governor of Kerala and many other dignitaries were attending that event, there were major security measures in place. This police officer had never seen Amma before in person, nor was he a devotee. He was just there on official duty.

As soon as he saw Amma, he forgot all protocol. He threw away his cap, removed his shoes and fell at Amma's feet. Normally a police officer will not do such thing in the presence of his superiors without obtaining their permission. This man didn't follow any protocol. Such was the impact of Amma's presence on him. He had no spiritual background and was well known for his harsh behavior. If such a hard-edged police officer can feel Amma's love and compassion at first sight and undergo a transformation, it should be easier for us.

Amma's love is not confined to humanity alone but embraces the entire animate world. During the period of Her intense *sadhana* (spiritual practices), dogs, cats, cows, goats, snakes, squirrels and birds all sought Her company and became Her intimate friends. At the time when Amma's own kith and kin had abandoned Her and were staunchly opposed to Her spiritual life, it was these animals that stood by Her at all times, regardless of the weather, and rendered Her their service.

When Amma was hungry, a dog would bring Her something to eat or the eagles would drop fish at the place where Amma was sitting. One day after a long meditation Amma felt very thirsty. When Amma opened Her eyes, a cow was standing next to Her in such a position that She could easily drink milk from its udders. Actually, the cow had been seen running from a house which was about six kilometers away. When Amma would be in prolonged *samadhi* (a transcendental state in which one loses all sense of individual identity), snakes would coil around Her body to bring Her awareness back to the normal plane. When Amma would fall unconscious fervently praying to Devi, a dog would rub against Her body and lick Her face and limbs in order to revive Her.

When Amma was asked about such incidents, She said, "When one gets rid of all attachments and aversion and attains equal vision, then even hostile animals will become friendly toward one."

Even nowadays we often witness animals and birds showing their feelings of friendship and intimacy with Amma.

Amma's all-encompassing maitri and total identification with the entire creation is amply revealed through Her refrain to Her children: "To truly love Amma is to love equally all beings in the world."

TRUTH VERSUS LOVE

Many of the villages near the ashram have many staunch communists and atheists. They never wanted an ashram to come up in the vicinity. In the early days of the ashram, they were trying their level best to destroy it any way they could. They would come in a group and protest, shout slogans and sometimes even throw stones into the ashram. There was one such incident when some of these rabble rousers came in a small group and started throwing stones at the ashram building. We were very angry, and we wanted to fight with them, but Amma said, "No, no, be quiet! Everything will be fine."

However, when one of the brahmacharis was hit by a small stone, Amma became upset. It pained Her heart to see this innocent boy who had taken refuge at Her feet come to even a little harm for no reason.

In the great Mahabharata War, there was an interesting incident of a clash between truth and love. Bhishma, the mighty military chieftain of the Kauravas, was a great devotee of Krishna. Circumstances forced him fight against Arjuna who was also devoted to Krishna and was under the Lord's protection. Krishna had declared that he would not take up arms in the war but would only be the charioteer of Arjuna. Hearing the vow of the Lord, Bhishma made another vow. He vowed that he would make the Lord take up arms. So he fought fiercely with Arjuna and Krishna. When arrows were shot at Krishna, he was not at all disturbed. He bore the wounds with a sweet smile. Having failed to tempt the Lord to take up arms to fight, Bhishma changed his strategy. He started showering arrows on Arjuna who, though a powerful warrior, could not match the skill and experience of the old chieftain. Incapable of protecting himself from the rain of arrows, Arjuna sought the protection of Krishna. Now Krishna could no longer remain a mere witness. The Lord, who is the embodiment of Truth, was ready to break his promise. Krishna jumped from the chariot and charged toward Bhishma with his weapon. Bhishma was happy to see the angry mood of the Lord who, in order to uphold the vow of one devotee and save the life of another, was ready to incur the disgrace and ill fame of having broken his own vow. As soon as Krishna started to run toward Bhishma, Bhishma dropped all his weapons and prostrated to Krishna. The love of a Master for His or Her disciple is so great that the Master will go to any extent to save the disciple. Likewise, if somebody hurts Amma, She doesn't mind at all; but when any of Her devotees are harmed in any way, She cannot tolerate it. Out of compassion, a great soul like Amma often mitigates people's negative karma. Even when a Mahatma punishes someone, and even if that punishment is severe, it is always for the ultimate well-being of that person; it is an act of grace.

Amma's way of dealing with the man who had thrown the stone at the brahmachari was not to mitigate his karma. She just allowed nature to take its own course. And so he had to suffer the full consequences of his own actions. A few days after the incident, the house belonging to that man was completely destroyed by lightning. He had to move elsewhere for his livelihood.

Amma explains, "I never punish anybody. If I am abused or harassed, I don't care at all. But when a devotee suffers such abuse, even God will not forgive the perpetrator. Everyone has to experience the fruits of his or her actions. There is no other way."

There are people who are so egoistic, arrogant and wicked that they will not admit or recognize the greatness of Mahatmas. This has always been the case; there were those who opposed Rama, Krishna, Jesus and other Masters as well.

However, there are also hundreds of thousands of people who have been transformed by Amma's unconditional love and compassion. There was a newly married couple who came to the ashram to stay with Amma. Someone asked the couple, "Why do you want to come to see Amma? You are newly married and could have gone for a honeymoon."

They said, "We want to experience Amma's love." Generally, a couple feels maximum love toward each other during the initial period of their marriage and honeymoon. Even at that time this couple wanted to experience Amma's love. So there is something sublime, something divine, in Amma's love that cannot be equaled by the love we get from any other source. That is why it is able to bring about such tremendous transformation in our lives. Even the animals and plants respond to this radiant sunshine of Her love.

A few years ago, a devotee from Chennai offered a baby elephant to Amma. The elephant was only one and a half years old when he came to the ashram. Amma named him Ram. For the first few weeks he would often cry, especially during the night. When everyone else was enjoying deep sleep, Ram was crying because he missed his mother. (He had already been separated from his mother, and there was no way he could be reunited with her.) His crying would often wake us up.

One night he cried more than usual and did not eat properly. Some of us informed Amma about this. Amma said, "If he keeps crying, bring him to me." Ram started crying again. The brahmachari who was one of those in charge of looking after Ram did not want to disturb Amma by taking Ram to Her, even though Amma had instructed him to do so. When Ram kept crying, Amma came out of Her room and asked some brahmacharis to bring him into the yard in front of Amma's room. Ram was brought to Amma, and She started lovingly stroking his trunk and forehead. She also fed him some bananas and biscuits. Amma kept asking him questions, like "Ram, are you sad? Do you like the ashram? Do you like Amma? Do you like your brothers and sisters here?" She asked such questions as though Ram were able to understand. Amma kept stroking him for at least half an hour with a great deal of love and care. Then She told the brahmacharis to tie Ram to the tree which was by the side of Her room.

It seemed that Amma's love and affection made him so happy that he no longer missed his own mother. He cried during a few more nights, but then Amma would ask for him to be brought to Her and would spend some time with him, stroking him and feeding him. After a few days he stopped crying totally. I am sure that he was feeling his own mother's love and presence through Amma.

Now Ram is almost four years old. After the evening bhajans, Amma regularly spends some time playing with

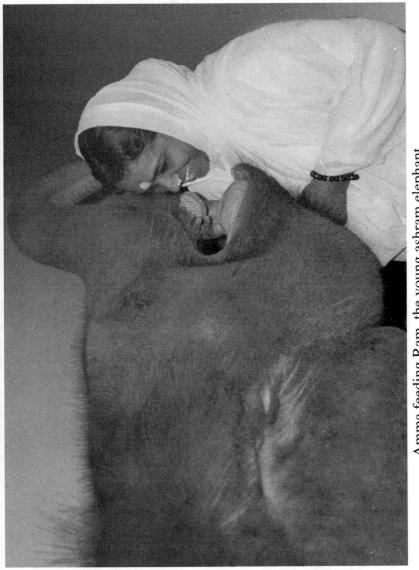

Amma feeding Ram, the young ashram elephant

Amma consecrating the Madurai Brahmasthanam temple

him, feeding him and talking to him. If Amma doesn't do that, Ram becomes very sad. Sometimes he is naughty and the mahouts (caretakers) will not be able to pacify him, but Amma is always able to calm him down.

SUBTLE SENSITIVITY

When negative qualities increase in people, naturally their actions will be detrimental to the universal harmony. When this harmony is disturbed, calamities can occur.

We are not able to feel this disharmony because our minds are not subtle enough. However, we can recognize the effect. Earthquakes, cyclones, floods, and other such natural calamities are all symptoms of this disharmony. In earlier years there was more harmony and fewer disasters. Now the situation has changed. Natural calamities have become a common occurrence. Although we can't feel the disharmony in the cosmos, Mahatmas like Amma can feel it.

When Amma decided to build an ashram in Madurai, She asked me to find land on which to build. With the help of the local devotees there, I found what I thought was a good piece of land for a good price. On our way back from Amma's programs in Chennai (then called Madras), as requested by me, Amma chose to stop and bless the land. But when I took Amma to see it, She threw Her arms up in the air and exclaimed, "Oh, God! My Madurai children's money is going to sink into the mud!" The other devotees who were present and I were upset when we heard

Amma's reaction. My mind wasn't subtle enough to feel the negative vibrations there. But Amma could feel it right away.

Upon investigation we discovered that no one wanted this piece of land; that was why we were able to purchase it for such a good price. The land was right off one of the major highways of Tamil Nadu; that particular stretch of the road was infamous for the odd number of fatal accidents that occurred there. Head-on collisions and cars rolling over were common; buses had even overturned there, and many people had lost their lives. On top of that, several people had hanged themselves from a particular tree nearby.

From the very beginning the construction was plagued with uncanny difficulties. Once, the tent housing all the cement and paint supplies somehow caught fire, and all the supplies were lost. So many times we would find that a wall or some other structure had not been built according to the plan; it would have to be torn down and re-built. Whole teams of workers would quit after just a week's work, simply saying they didn't want to return to that place. We had never experienced these problems in the construction of any other ashram. Normally, it took six months for us to build a branch ashram. The Madurai ashram took three years to complete and cost three times as much as we had expected. Amma's prediction had been 100% correct.

After three years of construction, Amma said that She wanted to consecrate the temple even though the work was rest of the construction went smoothly and there have not been any problems since. In fact, the once infamous stretch of road passing by the ashram is now famous for another reason - there has not been a single accident along the same curve that saw so many fatal accidents. The nearby tree that people had hanged themselves from was blown down in a storm. The once forlorn, desolate surrounding area is now full of houses, shops and other establishments. By Her sankalpa (divine resolve), Amma transformed a curse into a blessing. Someone asked Amma why She had chosen such an accursed, unwanted spot to build Her temple. Amma replied that She chooses such places so that the negative vibrations in that place can be converted into positive vibrations.

It is not only negative vibrations that Amma is so sensitive to. Once we asked Amma to take us to Tiruvan-namalai, a holy shrine in Tamil Nadu. In the van on the way there, Amma was telling jokes and stories. There was one brahmachari who fell asleep, and Amma poured some water into his mouth and put something in his nose. She was playing with us like this while the vehicle was passing through a village. Suddenly She became very serious. She closed Her eyes and held Her hands in mudras (gestures with spiritual significance). For about 10 or 15 minutes She was sitting in a meditative mood. Everyone fell silent. Then She opened Her eyes and after a few minutes started talking again. We didn't know why She had done this. Soon after that we stopped for tea. Seeing our group in white clothes and wearing long hair and beards, some people who were standing by the roadside asked us whether we were from the ashram of a swami in a nearby village. We had never heard of that swami.

Some of us became curious about that swami, and asked about him and his ashram. They said that about twenty miles from the village where we were, there was an avadhut (saint whose behavior does not conform to social norms) who looks like a beggar and lives in solitude, scarcely talking except to utter strange words and sounds. Then we remembered that that was almost the same place where Amma suddenly went into a meditative mood.

Later, Amma said that She had felt the strong vibrations of compassion around that place.

These incidents show us how sensitive Amma is. I had neither been able to feel the negative vibrations of the land I had chosen, nor the positive vibrations emanating from the avadhut and his ashram. But Amma experienced both without being told anything about the places. Similarly, Amma will know any disturbance in the world. She can feel and perceive anything in the universe without actually being there physically.

CHAPTER 5

THE IMPORTANCE OF HAVING A GURU

WHY WE NEED A GURU

"Even though the wind blows everywhere,
we enjoy coolness only under the shade of a tree.
Similarly, a Guru is necessary for us who live
in the scorching heat of worldly existence."

— Amma

Many people wonder why we need a Guru at all. Even if we want to learn something as simple as the alphabet, we need the help of a teacher. If we need a teacher to learn just 26 symbols, what can be said about mastering the complexities of spiritual life?

Take the instance of someone traveling to a place he or she hasn't been before. They may have a road map to reach that destination, but along the way the roads may be in poor condition, there may be a section frequented by highway robbers, there may be a detour, or there may be wild animals. Such details will not be included on the map. To reach the destination safely, our traveler needs the guidance of someone who has already traveled this route.

Similarly, to travel along the spiritual path, we need a guide who knows the goal, knows all the twists and turns and pitfalls along the path, and knows our strengths and weaknesses. In Amma we have the supreme guide to the spiritual path. Not only does She know the way, She is willing to walk alongside us, holding our hands at every step of the way and illuminating the path ahead.

Spiritual practices can be compared to a tonic. Taken in the correct dosage, it will be good for our health. But if we take too much, it can cause unexpected problems. Similarly, spiritual practices, done in the right way and in the right proportion to our constitution, will give us mental and physical health. But if we overdo it, it can lead to problems. Only a Satguru can properly judge what is the best spiritual prescription for each person.

A woman who was very overweight bought a book on how to lose weight. The book suggested different types of medicine. She selected one for which the prescription read, "Take one pill, then skip a day, take one the next day, then skip a day. Continue for six months."

After just three months, the woman had already lost 100 pounds. But she had started to suffer from headaches, muscle fatigue and dehydration. This concerned her, and she finally decided to see a doctor. The doctor was shocked to hear about how much weight she had lost in such a short time. "Obviously the treatment is working," he said. "But maybe these symptoms are side-effects of the pills you're taking."

"Oh, no, the pills are fine," the woman said. "It's the skipping that's killing me!"

We can also see the importance of having a Guru by looking at the lives of *Avatars* (divine incarnations who come back to the world just to help others) such as Rama and Krishna. Though they were born with the knowledge of the Supreme and had no need for a Guru as such, they became disciples in order to demonstrate to the world the greatness of the Guru.

THE MEANING OF "GURU"

The Vedas, the most ancient texts and most subtle spiritual treasures of humanity, begin with the invocation of fire, "*Agnimeele purohitam...*" The word *agni* (fire) in that verse refers to the pure Consciousness that illumines everything. It also represents the Guru, as the syllable "gu" means darkness and "ru" means removal. Thus the word Guru conveys the meaning, "fire that dispels the darkness within." The darkness within is the darkness of ignorance.

I have also heard Amma saying that God-realized souls can take on others' karma and burn it in the fire of their own Self-knowledge.

Guru has another wonderful meaning: "heavy." Heavy not as in weight, for if it were so, there would be many people who have the qualification to be a Guru! A real Master is heavy by means of His or Her spiritual glory and greatness. In Indian astrology, the largest and heaviest planet, Jupiter, is called the Guru planet. Lord Krishna, though only a cowherd boy, was considered as the universal Guru because of this quality of spiritual greatness. In the *Srimad Bhagavatam*, it is said that only seven people really knew who Krishna was during His lifetime. It was only after their lifetime that many great ones like Krishna, Rama, and Jesus were widely accepted as Avatars. We should recognize how lucky we are that we know that our Amma is divine even while She is in the body. It is a testament to Amma's compassion that She allows so many of us to experience Her divinity and greatness.

Most of us can say we have been given many wonderful experiences with Amma. However, if one of our demands does not materialize, we forget all about our previous experiences. When we show our devotion, if Amma doesn't appear to reciprocate, at times we might think that Amma doesn't care about us anymore, or that She doesn't know about our love for Her. In fact, Amma wants us to develop our faith and inner strength. She cannot continue playing to our whims and fancies forever. Amma says, "Whenever you have doubts, recollect your previous experiences with the Guru and remember the ways in which you have experienced the greatness and compassion of the Guru. Think about those experiences and try to strengthen your faith." Holding onto such experiences and incidents, we should try to progress along the spiritual path.

A SOURCE OF SPIRITUAL UNDERSTANDING

Science and technology have impacted our lives tremendously. The inventions, gadgets and comforts we enjoy today could not even have been conceived of just a few decades ago. Yet, the restlessness and misery of the human psyche has also escalated proportionately.

Statistics show that thousands of people commit suicide every year. This is not a small number. People do not know how to find contentment in life. They try to find relief in material possessions, relationships, entertainment, alcohol and drugs, etc., and when all these fail, some turn to suicide. To such people, life is miserable because they cannot find lasting happiness anywhere. Today the standards of living have gone up in many parts of the world, but what about the quality of life? The increase of suicide, crime and riots is just a symptom of the decline in psychological well-being.

Two generations ago suicide, drug addiction and psychiatric problems were much less common. Belief in God or a divine power guiding our life was also much more prevalent. It was the belief in God and the resulting commitment to a values-based life that helped those earlier generations overcome miseries and find balance.

When we are happy, healthy and wealthy, we think we don't need God. That perspective is wrong. God is not an emergency kit. Remembrance of God is needed for our mental and emotional well-being. This principle is reflected by the peace and happiness we can feel after performing just a little spiritual practice.

Amma says that life is a mixture of pleasure and pain and that spirituality teaches us how to maintain equanimity of mind in all circumstances. Only then can we lead a peaceful life. Without spirituality guiding our thoughts and actions, any small problem can affect us deeply. What can we do to remain unaffected? Amma gives an example:

There is a place where people are setting off firecrackers. If a person who knows about this happens to pass through the area, he or she will not be jolted by the sound of an explosion. On the other hand, a person who doesn't know what is happening and who isn't prepared for it will be shocked when the firecrackers suddenly explode nearby. Similarly, a person who understands the nature of the world will not be shocked by sudden calamities.

For everything in life, a spiritual foundation is necessary. Compassion, love, and selflessness should be present in all relationships. Unless people have an inner foundation of spirituality and associated values, they cannot maintain a loving relationship. During modern times, so many marriages are breaking apart. What a difference it would make if each husband and wife would forgive and forget each other's faults.

When a person goes to a counselor or a psychiatrist for a problem such as depression, the professional will advise the patient to relax and to practice positive thinking, meditation, etc. in order to overcome the depression. Some psychiatrists don't refer to the treatment as meditation but use another name such as "creative visualization."

As saints and sages have said for millennia, turning toward God and following spiritual practices helps us to develop values that offer peace of mind despite our complex and changing world. One need only follow the advice of the Masters to prevent depression and avoid becoming a psychiatric patient.

AN EXAMPLE OF SELFLESS LOVE

The scriptures say, "*Atmanastu kamaya sarvam priyam bavathi*," which means, "It is for the sake of our own happiness that we like objects and other people." We love other people and objects as long as they make us happy. The unfortunate basis for this truth is that we love ourselves more than we love others. Almost everyone is looking for love while very few are ready to give love without expecting anything in return. If we are expecting something when we give our love, it cannot be called pure love. Rather, it is a business deal motivated by profit. This is unfortunate, because love is not a consumer product having a specific market value. What is traded in the name of love is not love at all. It is like a plastic fruit which is pleasing to the eye but cannot nourish our body and soul.

A man who is unhappy thinks he will find joy if he gets married, and a woman believes that if she marries, her unhappiness will disappear. So one unhappy person marries another. There will just be two unhappy people living together. They may be happy for a limited time, but problems will surface.

Many wives and husbands fight and separate. Initially they loved each other so much. During the honeymoon each of them may say, "I cannot live without you even for a moment." After a few years the feeling is reversed: "I cannot live with you even for a moment."

This is the nature of worldly love. It is always based on expectations, and when these expectations are not fulfilled, the love ceases to exist. It can even turn into hate. Unconditional love is what we all want, but we receive only conditional love. The husband and wife love each other in the beginning but ultimately the love deteriorates, because it was built on selfish motives. Once the charm of novelty withers away, both find that they are not satisfied with the love they are receiving from the other person.

Amma always says, "When there is mutual love, understanding and trust, our problems and worries will decrease. When these qualities are absent, problems will increase. Love is the foundation of a happy life. Knowingly or unknowingly, we are disregarding this truth. Just as our bodies need proper food to live and grow, our souls need love to grow properly. The strength and nourishment that love can give to our souls is even more potent than the nourishing power of a mother's milk for a baby."

Amma tells us to love others but not to expect anything in return, and we should work toward that goal. We can see this selfless love in a Self-realized Master. He or She doesn't expect anything from anyone.

HEALING PRESENCE

We may have many problems in our personal life, but when we are in the presence of a Satguru like Amma, our minds become calm and our worries melt away. I have seen many people come to Amma with questions and doubts, but the moment they rest in Her lap or are embraced by Her, everything vanishes from their minds. After darshan they realize they have forgotten to ask their questions. They often find that their once crucial problems are no longer disturbing their minds at all. At some level, a transformation has taken place. This is the benefit of being in Amma's divine presence.

When Amma was in Chicago in 1993 at the Parliament of World's Religions Centennial, She was requested to give the closing prayers and message. The devotees brought the car close to the stage door so that Amma would be able to get to the car as quickly as possible when the function was over; otherwise, people would crowd around Her. As the Dalai Lama and some other important celebrities were also on the stage along with Amma, there was tight security. Because of this, it was difficult to get permission to park the car near the stage door. Amma finished Her prayer and message and was walking out the stage door toward the car when She saw a security guard arguing with a devotee. The guard's face was red with anger and his voice was escalating. Amma walked straight up to the guard, stroked his chest and gave him a hug. He was totally taken aback by this unexpected loving and soothing embrace.

The guard, who had been insisting that due to security reasons they should move the car and bring Amma only through the designated gate and not through any other door, was now escorting Amma to the car and opening the door for Her! Just one touch was enough to change him. Next year when Amma came to Chicago, he was the first person in the darshan line.

When a flower has fully blossomed, whoever is passing by it will receive the gift of the flower's fragrance. Likewise, Amma is overflowing with love, compassion and grace. Whoever goes near Her will naturally benefit.

Once I visited the home of one of Amma's devotees. There was a teenage girl in the house whose room was full of indecent pictures. Her parents were staunch devotees of Amma, but the girl refused to meet Amma. The girl's mother was very upset. The next year, this same girl knelt before Amma and wept profusely. As soon as she returned home she removed all the indecent pictures from her room. Not long thereafter, when I visited their home, I saw only two pictures in the girl's room. One was a picture of Amma and the other was a photo of the girl with Amma. Nobody ever told her to remove the other pictures—she did it on her own.

Overcoming our likes, dislikes, and negative tendencies is very difficult, but in the presence of a Great Master like Amma, it becomes much easier. It can even happen spontaneously.

AN EXPRESSION OF GOD'S COMPASSION

na me pārthā 'sti kartavyaṁ triṣu lokeṣu kiṁcana
nā 'navāptam avāptavyaṁ varta eva ca karmaṇi

*I have no duty to perform, nor is there anything in the
three worlds unattained which is to be attained, still I am
engaged in action.*

—*Bhagavad Gita*, Chapter III, Verse 22

Amma says that Mahatmas are carriers of God's compassion and the vehicles of God's grace. Some scriptures say that the Mahatmas are even more compassionate than God because they come to the world for no other reason than to help us and uplift us. They have already achieved what has to be achieved with the human birth. They are full and complete. They don't want anything except to give. They could be in a constant state of infinite bliss. Instead, they choose to leave that state of bliss and descend to our plane of awareness in order to help us.

Amma says, "My only aim is to make My children happy in this birth and in all the births to come." Amma listens to the problems of thousands of people, day and night. She has been doing this for the past 30 years. So far, Amma has personally met, hugged and listened to the problems and difficulties of more than 23 million people. No other example needs to be mentioned to prove the extent of Her compassion. Amma has no need to do this; She does it for our sake.

Though Amma never feels sad for Herself, She feels sad and upset when Her devotees are sad. She is as hard as a diamond, but when it comes to Her children, She is as soft as a flower. Our sorrows are reflected in Her mind, and She is moved by them. Amma's life is only for the sake of those who seek Her help.

If we pray to Her wholeheartedly, everything will be taken care of by Amma. Many problems will be resolved, and we will be given the strength and the courage to accept and face those that remain. When you come to a Mahatma, life's complexities seem to simplify.

There was a couple in India who had only one son. The parents were deeply religious, and they advised their son to pray to God, but he never paid any attention to their words. He had never prayed to God in his life. One day he was offered a job in the Middle East, and he decided to accept it. His parents, who were devotees of Amma, asked him see Amma before he left because he was going to a distant land and would return only after two or three years. They asked him to take all his documents to the ashram so that Amma could bless them. Because he didn't want to disobey his parents and upset them before his departure, he decided to go and see Amma.

He went to the ashram the next day with all his documents—his passport, visa and appointment order to be blessed. When he went for darshan, Amma asked him, "Are you going to take this job?" The boy said, "Yes." Amma didn't say anything after that. She closed Her eyes for a few moments and then blessed him.

On his way back home, he was traveling in a bus. He was so tired that he fell asleep. When he opened his eyes, he found that his briefcase containing his documents was missing. He was in a state of shock and disbelief. Soon these feelings turned into total rage. As soon as he got out of the bus, he ran home like a mad man. He almost beat up his parents as he thought his whole life had been ruined because of them. He told them it was their fault to have sent him to see Amma, as a result of which he had now lost everything. His parents were also very upset. They didn't know how to answer their son or how to console him.

The very next day, the parents came to see Amma and tearfully told Her what had happened to their son the previous day. They also told Amma that they had come without their son's knowledge. Amma told them not to worry and that everything would be all right. Not long thereafter, the Gulf War broke out. It was in Iraq that this boy and others he knew had been given a job, and some of his friends were already there. The building where he was supposed to have worked was bombed. Many people died, and some of his friends were seriously injured.

Some time later, the local police station called the boy to say that they had found his briefcase. The thief seemed to have been a relatively good person; he had taken the money and some other valuables that were useful to him and left the briefcase on the roadside near the police station without tampering with or damaging the travel and other documents. Someone who found this abandoned briefcase promptly delivered it to the police.

When Amma was told what had happened, She said, "I knew what was going to happen, but if I had asked him not to accept the job, he would not have listened to Me, and if he had gone there to work, he would definitely have been seriously injured or even killed. This was the only way his life could be saved."

Later, the boy was offered a good job through Amma's grace, but by that time he actually wanted to join the ashram! This is what his parents had been praying for.

Many of Amma's devotees have the experience of Amma personally helping them. Of course, whenever we are able to give a heartfelt call to Amma, She will respond. When we are really in trouble, our call to God will be very sincere and wholehearted. When we are happy and pray to God, there may be less sincerity in our prayer. When we are suffering, our call to God will have more depth and devotion. God sometimes gives us problems in life just so that we don't forget to reach out sincerely to Him.

There is an ardent devotee of Amma in Mumbai who was diagnosed as having four blocks in his heart. The doctors decided he should undergo open-heart surgery. He was very frightened and upset about this. His sons were also very worried, so they called the ashram and informed Amma. The father was crying to Amma over the phone, mostly out of fear. Amma told him, "Don't worry, My son, everything will be all right." Amma sent Her *prasad*[5] to this devotee through another devotee who was going to Mumbai the next day.

Two days before the surgery, the chief surgeon decided to do one last test before the operation. To the doctor's utter surprise, he found that there was now only one minor block. The chief surgeon consulted with his colleagues and then decided that it was not necessary to do the surgery immediately. The devotee was discharged after being given some medicines and some dietary instruction. He went home happily, thanking Amma profusely.

It is almost eight years now since this miracle took place, and so far the need has not arisen for him to undergo the bypass surgery.

A sincere call can work wonders, especially when we have a living Master. Instead of spending our life in meaningless pursuits, we should try to do the things in life that will bring us God's grace. Without God's grace, life is dry and empty. Let us try to use our time, energy, talents and physical capabilities to earn this grace.

AN OPPORTUNITY TO EXPERIENCE GOD

It is a tremendous opportunity to be in contact with a Mahatma. We may have faith in God, but it is difficult to have a close relationship with God because it is not possi-

---

[5] *Prasad* is anything blessed by the Guru or offered to a deity, usually food.

ble to see Him or communicate with Him directly. In a Mahatma's presence, we can feel and experience God because a Mahatma is always established in God-consciousness; such a person is one with God.

The bond that we establish with a Mahatma will always be in our heart, and we can feel His or Her protection around us. Like a mother hen protecting her chicks under her wing, Amma protects Her children wherever they are.

One evening, Amma and the brahmacharis were sitting on the sand on the side of the ashram closest to the back-waters. Amma suddenly closed Her eyes and went into deep meditation. After some time when Amma opened Her eyes, one brahmachari asked Her, "Amma, whom do you meditate on?" Amma replied that She thinks of Her children during this time, and in a subtle way goes to those who are praying to Amma with a yearning heart. Amma later said that at that time a lady devotee of Amma, whose husband opposed her visiting the ashram, was crying bitterly before Amma's picture in her shrine room. We later heard from that devotee that She had had a vision of Amma at that time and had been greatly consoled to find that Amma is with her even in her house.

It is the company of a Great Master that helps us to make our mind strong. The Master's love enables us to accept everything that comes our way and to face the challenges in our life. We are extremely fortunate to have God, incarnated as the Divine Mother Amma, living among us.

We don't really have to worry about anything, for we can be assured that Amma is always taking care of us. Whenever a problem arises in our lives, it is reassuring to know that Amma is aware of it and that She will offer help and support. This conviction gives us great relief and comfort. A child-like innocent trust and love toward the Master is the beginning of our spiritual evolution.

Amma is trying to kindle spiritual awareness and positive qualities like love and compassion in us. She sets an example by the way She lives Her life.

Every one of us has these qualities within. For example, even a hardened criminal becomes filled with love when seeing his or her own child. A Mahatma creates situations to help us cultivate and manifest these loving qualities. When such love awakens in us, negative qualities are gradually removed.

Many of us came to Amma to get Her blessings for fulfillment of a desire or to obtain a solution to a problem. Amma says that through yearning for a higher goal, desires for lesser goals can be conquered. When we are with a Satguru, we can overcome many of our desires through our love for Him or Her. Because of the desire to live with Amma in the ashram, many of us are able to give up the desire for worldly things.

We should be able to maintain a living relationship, a close rapport with God. Amma used to tell us that during Her period of sadhana, She would earnestly pray to Devi to reveal Herself and She would occasionally get angry with Devi for not giving Her darshan.

If we can develop such intimacy with God and are able to direct all our emotions and feelings toward God, we can rid ourselves of all our negative tendencies. Amma says, "If you feel angry, direct your anger toward God. If you feel sad, direct your sorrow toward God. Sit before your altar or enter your shrine room and tell everything you have in your heart to God—just as a small child opens up before its mother. This will greatly unburden your heart and restore peace and calmness within."

A CHANCE TO LEARN ABOUT OURSELVES

We all have many disturbances in our minds. As soon as we come to a true Master, it may seem that the Master also contributes to those disturbances—as though the ones we have are not enough! The Guru will create certain situations for us and will tell us, "See, this is your problem." In this way the Guru will make us aware of the negativity within ourselves. This is an important part of the Guru's work. We need to be aware of our defects in order to correct them.

We rarely want to accept our own faults and weaknesses; instead, we tend to blame someone else. The mind at times is very negative. Sometimes, even if we have the best Guru available in the world, we project our negativities and defects onto the Guru and blame the Guru for our inadequacies. We may even leave the Guru thinking, "This is not a suitable Guru for me. I'm going to search for another Guru."

We've always had these disturbances, but only now are we slowly becoming aware of them. We think, "Before coming to Amma, I was really a very nice person, perhaps even saintly. Now that I've come to Amma, so many negativities are arising within me." Naturally we think there's something wrong with Amma. Such is our judgmental nature. The Guru creates situations just to make us aware that we have these defects; and then the Guru helps us to overcome them.

When we observe our mind superficially, we may think we don't have any negative *vasanas* (latent tendencies). But as we begin to dive deep into the mind, we find numerous negativities and desires. Amma gives an example to illustrate this point. A room may appear to be clean superficially, but when we start scrubbing it with soap and water, we can see there is still a lot of dirt. For our negative vasanas to come to the surface where we can see them, a suitable situation or environment is needed, and a true Master knows how to create just such situations. Amma gives the example of a snake in hibernation. While hibernating, a snake won't react to anything, but as soon as it wakes up it will react to the slightest provocation.

Swami Amritatmananda, one of Amma's senior disciples, tells a story from his early days as Amma's disciple that shows how She brings our negative qualities to the surface. Once, in an effort to stand out, he asked Amma what he felt was a tough question in front of a group of householders and brahmacharis. But Amma simply replied, "Dear child, you wouldn't understand the answer!"

In the past, Amma had frequently praised Swami Amritatmananda (then Ramesh Rao), saying that he had a lot of discrimination. Now, this criticism was too much for him to bear. He was so upset that he decided to go to Kanyakumari (the southern tip of India, a pilgrimage destination 200 kilometers away) for two days, as a protest.

Wandering around Kanyakumari, he found himself near the ashram of the avadhut Mayiamma. Mayiamma wasn't there at that time; a devotee had taken her to visit another city. As Swami Amritatmananda watched the sunset, his heart aching, one of Mayiamma's devotees approached him. Holding out a food-vessel, the devotee gestured to a pack of dogs lying nearby and said, "These creatures haven't even drunk any water because they cannot see Mayiamma. I've tried my best to coax them to eat. If you offer this food, perhaps they will eat it." Swami Amritatmananda followed his gaze. About fifty dogs were lying on the ground, their legs outstretched, with their chins on the ground and their eyes closed. Tear streaks stained the faces of most of them. Wonderstruck, he looked back at the man. Without pausing, the devotee continued, "When Mayiamma isn't here, these creatures don't eat anything. Do such beings exist?"

With the food-vessel in hand, Swami Amritatmananda approached the dogs. But the dogs didn't respond; they didn't even open their eyes. Without even stirring, they continued to lie there, as if in samadhi. After some time, four or five of the dogs looked up at him and then resumed their original posture. He could only wonder: how did these dogs acquire such dispassion? What priceless treasure had the dogs gained from Mayiamma?

His mind flew to Amritapuri. A glittering picture of Amma smiling affectionately and compassionately at him, beckoning him to come to Her, appeared before him, and then vanished. Losing control, he cried out loudly, "Amma!" Handing the food-vessel to the middle-aged man, he left and returned to Amritapuri as quickly as he could.

When he reached the ashram in the wee hours of the morning, he saw Amma sitting on the verandah of the *kalari* (small temple). He prostrated before Her and then stood close by, feeling guilty. Suddenly, a dog happened to walk by. Looking at it and speaking to no one in particular, Amma said, "Even dogs feel gratitude and love towards their masters." He looked carefully into Amma's eyes. They were brimming with tears. Overwhelmed by the hurt and guilt in his heart, he fell crying into Her lap. Amma kissed him compassionately on the head, and caressing him, She whispered, "My naughty child, has your anger disappeared?"

Having created the situation that causes our negative reaction, the Master points out our negative vasanas and shortcomings. Even in the face of this evidence, we often try to justify our reactions because we hate to admit that we have made a mistake.

Amma tells a joke in this regard. A man slipped and fell. When his wife teased him about it, the husband responded, "What's so funny? I'm just practicing my *yogasanas* (hatha yoga postures)! "

Through the love and patience of a true Master, we finally come to realize the truth about ourselves; we become aware of our negative tendencies and we change ourselves. However, Amma says that being in the physical presence of the Guru is not enough. We have to be open and allow the Guru to mold us, though this process can be painful. The stronger the vasana, the greater the pain will be; but if we really love our Guru, we won't feel that pain as we are being molded.

A man went to an eye doctor to have his eyes tested. The doctor asked him to read the letters on a board, using different lenses. But the patient wasn't able to read any of the letters, not even through the most powerful lens. The doctor got irritated and yelled, "Why can't you read any of those letters even with the most powerful lens?"

The patient coolly replied, "Because I still have to learn the alphabet."

Likewise, just as we have to know the alphabet to be able to read the letters of the alphabet, we have to be open in order to be able to appreciate the Guru's greatness. Only with an open heart can we receive the Guru's grace.

THE VALUE OF PRASAD

I remember an incident that took place many years ago when Amma visited the house of a devotee. I was still working in a bank at that time. When I finished work that evening, I went straight to the house Amma was visiting. I arrived at about nine o'clock.

In those days, Amma often visited the houses of devotees, many of whom were very poor. Amma would lovingly accept whatever *bhiksha* (offering) they placed before Her. As fish was much cheaper than vegetables, rice and fish were usually the main staples in the diet of the poor in that area. Amma, Herself, was a strict vegetarian; but out of compassion, She would eat whatever food these people offered Her, because She didn't want to hurt them or trouble them in any way.

When I arrived at the house that evening, Amma had just started eating with the devotees. As soon as She saw me, She gave me a handful of food. I took it respectfully, but when I looked at it, I saw a big chunk of fish!

I was born and brought up in a family that adhered to a strict vegetarian diet. So, when I saw the piece of fish, I immediately dropped it. I felt disgusted. Amma asked, "Why did you throw that away? It is prasad."

I said, "I don't want it because it's fish!" Although I was bothered by the smell of the fish, somehow I sat there until Amma finished eating.

Because of my loathing for the smell of fish, I threw up a few minutes later. After I finished vomiting, I reached for a bowl of water that was next to Amma. I didn't know that after eating the fish, She had washed Her hands in that water. Finding no other source of water, I just grabbed the bowl and started washing my face and rinsing my mouth. When Amma saw this, She smiled mischievously. I didn't know why She was smiling. A few others sitting around Amma started laughing, thinking that I was about to have a nightmarish experiencing from tasting fishy water and washing my face with it.

I used all the water, and as I rinsed with it, I discovered that the water smelled like pure rosewater. The fragrance was lovely—a great relief to me after the smell of that fish!

By that time everyone had finished eating, and the dishes were removed. But still I felt that there was a smell of fish coming from somewhere. I then noticed, to my surprise, that the fishy smell was coming from the stuff I had vomited. I couldn't believe it because I hadn't eaten any fish. So I understood there was something "fishy" about the whole situation!

One would have expected that the water in the bowl in which Amma had washed Her hands would smell like fish. Instead, it emitted the most wonderful fragrance of roses, while the stuff vomited by me, a strict vegetarian, smelled of fish, even though I hadn't eaten any fish. I then realized that this was a lesson for me about disrespecting the Guru's prasad. When I threw the prasad away, I had forgotten to think of Amma as the Goddess. I looked upon Amma as an ordinary person and didn't consider the food given by Her as prasad. Whatever food the Guru gives is prasad. We should accept it wholeheartedly.

At that time, I had already been worshipping Amma for some time and had even had a vision of Her as the Goddess. This vision was elevating for a while and certainly reinforced my faith in Her, but I was still not able to sustain the conviction, at all times and in all circumstances, that Amma is one with the Divine Mother. If we can sustain this conviction continuously, we can perform all our actions with more love and dedication. Amma says that when we develop the attitude of dedication, one by one our negative tendencies will fade away.

AMMA'S OMNISCIENCE

Sometimes Amma would tell me the details about a person who has just joined the darshan line for the first time. When that person came up for darshan, Amma would ask that person all the details about him- or herself, which Amma had already told me. This happened a few times. Once, when this had just happened, I asked Amma out of curiosity, "Why did you ask him all those details which you already knew?" To this, Amma replied that She had done that just to make him say a few words to Her, so that he would feel some closeness with Her. So, in this way, Amma makes us feel close to Her, adding a more personal touch to the darshan. Because of this personal touch, remembering Amma's smile, Her words, Her touch, etc., is a good meditation for all of us. As She binds us with Her divine love, She inspires us to cultivate good qualities. Thus, Amma molds us into instruments that are fit to receive God's grace.

Occasionally, when we tell Amma about our sorrows, She sheds tears with us. This shows us that Amma is actually sharing our problems, and it means a great deal to us. If Amma didn't show any emotions, She'd be like a robot; nobody would feel any connection or closeness with Her. On the other hand, when we see Amma showing such human emotions, we tend to forget Her greatness and divinity.

In Australia, a five-year-old boy went with his mother to see a person who was giving a spiritual program. That person gave the boy a nice big apple. A month later when the boy's mother told him that they were going to meet an Indian saint called Amma, the boy immediately asked his mother, "Will Amma give me an apple like that other person did?" What could his mother say? She had not even met Amma. So she could only say, "I don't know."

They came to see Amma. After their darshan, they were walking away when Amma suddenly called the boy and handed him an apple. Many other children came to Amma that day, but Amma didn't give any of them an apple. It was only to this boy that She gave an apple. The boy was so happy. His mother shed tears of joy wondering how Amma could have known that her son had asked her about the apple.

When Swami Amritageetananda, one of Amma's senior disciples, first met Amma, he wanted to join Her ashram immediately; but Amma thought it would not be right as he was already enrolled in a Vedanta course at another ashram. She asked him to complete the course and only then seek permission to come to Her ashram. Though he felt sad, Amma reassured him, and said that he should write to Her and that She would reply.

When he returned to the ashram in Mumbai, he started writing letters to Amma. He sent seven letters altogether, but Amma did not write back.

Just before his course of study was to end, Swami Amritageetananda wrote to Amma again, telling Her that his instructors had agreed that he could join Amma's ashram after his course was completed. Still, Amma didn't reply. Because Amma never responded, he became convinced that She did not want him to join Her ashram. Not only that, he felt as if he had to leave the spiritual path altogether after the Vedanta course, for he had already announced his intention to leave the ashram where he was enrolled. He decided to return home and look for a job. As soon as the thought of the impending worldly life entered his mind, he stopped all his spiritual practices.

Three days later, he received a tiny letter. The small slip of paper was from Amma. It read, "Son, you have stopped your spiritual practices. Your mind is completely out of control. Resume your spiritual practices. Amma is with you." He felt a rush of joy at the realization that Amma had been with him every step of the way. He resumed his spiritual practices, completed the course and then joined Amma's ashram.

Swami Pranavamritananda, another of Amma's senior disciples, once had an experience which demonstrates how our minds are like an open book to Amma. He had seen a touching movie about Adi Shankaracharya, one of the greatest exemplars of Vedanta philosophy. It kindled in him a deep interest in meditation. He experimented with meditation and even visited some sannyasins in order to seek answers to his many questions about meditation. But they could not clarify his doubts.

One day, he went to visit his aunt who lived near the college he was attending. She was a devotee of Amma. As he walked into her house, he noticed a young lady dressed in white robes. In due time, seeing many people there whom he already knew to be devotees of Amma, it became clear to him who She was. Seeing Her youthful form, he thought, "What could this young lady know about anything?" He went to the adjacent room to escape from Her. Amma immediately entered that room, sat down next to him, and grabbing his arm, saying, "My son, I wanted to meet you and hear you sing." The other devotees then came one by one, and gathered around Amma. Without anyone's asking, Amma began to speak about meditation. Within a few moments' time, Amma not only cleared all of his doubts, but also gave him a very clear perspective about meditation. He was convinced about Her omniscience and felt that Her words were directed at him.

Swami Pranavamritananda recounts another incident which illustrates how Amma's omniscience catches our every mistake. A youth who used to visit the ashram often was once sitting behind Amma after darshan. He was enjoying being in Amma's presence. At the same time, he was also conscious of what everyone else was doing. He would wonder, watching them sit around Amma after receiving darshan, "Why are all these people just sitting around? Why don't they get up and do something worth-while?" Just at that moment, Amma turned to him and, looking him in the eye, said, "Get up and go to work, you idler!" Stunned by Amma's all-knowing nature, he jumped up and ran towards the kitchen—the right place to go—and did some work. Afterwards, he didn't forget to serve his stomach!

If we are aware that Amma knows everything about us—all our little wishes and secret desires—we can constantly remember Her and remain in tune with Her.

CHAPTER 6

AWAKENING AND DEVELOPING OUR SPIRITUAL POTENTIAL

UPLIFT YOURSELF WITH YOUR SELF

uddhared ātmanā'tmānaṁ nā'tmānam avasādayet
ātmai'va hy ātmano bandhurātmai'va ripur ātmanaḥ

Uplift yourself by your own Self.
Do not think badly about or condemn yourself.
The Self alone is your benefactor,
and the Self alone is your enemy.

— *Bhagavad Gita*, Chapter VI, Verse 5

Since consciousness is divine, don't ever denounce yourself whatever your situation may be. Let the whole world laugh at you, saying you are a total failure in life, but do not believe that. Don't have one iota of self-pity. You have infinite power within you. Holding on to that power of Truth, elevate yourself.

Everything related to Amma's life was challenging. Yet She faced each experience with courage and determination. Amma shows the way for all of us to realize our own divinity despite all the problems in our lives. Divinity is our birthright and our true nature. When we meet a Master like Amma, we become inspired to undertake a spiritual quest. A true Master helps us by being a constant source of inspiration.

Even though She was extraordinary within, Amma grew up like an ordinary village girl, with no particular advantages. She did not have a luxurious life, and She had to struggle every step of the way, but She persevered.

When Amma started giving darshan in Krishna Bhava and Devi Bhava, some people slandered Her for hugging people of the opposite sex. Because the villagers saw Her as an ordinary person, not as Krishna or Devi, they accused Her of misguiding the devotees in the name of devotion. But Amma continued to lovingly offer darshan, and today She hugs hundreds of thousands of devotees a year around the world.

When Amma consecrated the first Brahmasthanam Temple[6] in Kodungalloor, Kerala, religious scholars and priests took issue with the fact that a woman was consecrating a temple. Amma didn't give up. Today, there are seventeen such temples consecrated by Amma, and each one serves as a source of relief for the thousands of people who worship there.

---

[6] Born out of Amma's divine intuition, these unique temples are the first to show multiple deities on a single icon. The icon is four-sided, displaying Ganesha, Shiva, Devi and Rahu, emphasizing the inherent unity underlying the manifold aspects of the Divine.

It would have been so easy for Amma to abandon Her efforts at any step of the way and see Herself as a failure, but She didn't. She faced opposition and criticism without letting it affect Her mind. Instead, She was intent on carrying out Her mission. Her life is the best practical example for anyone to follow.

THE INSULATED MIND

During the early years, there were many people strongly opposed to Amma, even though She had never wronged them in any way. The villagers were ignorant of spirituality and ashram life. They were also jealous because they could not imagine how a village girl, who seemed to be one of them, could become so famous. People from all over India and from other parts of the world were coming to see Amma. Thus, out of this ignorance and jealousy, the local villagers started creating problems. Somehow, they wanted to get rid of Amma. Such was their hatred and opposition!

In those days Amma used to go to different houses to perform *pujas* (a ceremonial form of worship). Many families were suffering from the effects of black magic. The practitioners of those evil acts would imbue certain objects, such as a conch or a talisman, with evil spirits by using certain mantras. They would then bury the object in the front or back yard of the targeted house. Many such afflicted families would come to see Amma. She would help them by conducting a puja in their house, or She would go to a spot in the yard and ask the family members to dig there. When they uncovered the cursed object, they could dispose of it, thereby freeing themselves from the effects of the curse.

Actually, there was no need for Amma to do all this. If, in fact, black magic had been performed, Her sankalpa was enough to remove it. Sometimes, Amma would even take the effects of the curse upon Herself, thus saving the family members. But as some of Her devotees didn't have the strong faith that Amma could do such things just by Her will, Amma would go to their homes and perform pujas just to put their minds at ease.

Often when Amma went to such houses, there would be people mocking and taunting Her, and sometimes even throwing stones at Her. No one else could have faced that kind of opposition with such strength and equanimity of mind. Even when so many people were against Her, She was not disturbed in the least. When the mind is established in Supreme Truth, nothing can affect it. You'll be smiling even if someone tries to kill you. That is the greatness of being established in the Self. Amma is the perfect example of this truth.

In those days, Amma's parents used to scold Her harshly. Her parents were very strict because they had three other daughters who were yet to be married, and they were always afraid that the family would be given a bad name. At that time in India, especially in the villages, it was considered taboo for a young girl and boy to talk often with each other. If a teenage girl happened to spend too much time with a boy, the parents would get very upset. People would start spreading rumors about her. Nobody would marry that girl. Because of this, Amma's parents strongly insisted that as soon as the Devi Bhava was over, all of us boys should leave the ashram immediately. Nobody was allowed to stay there after the Devi Bhava. Amma used to feel sad whenever Her parents would chase us away. But there was nothing She could do about it because She was still living with Her parents.

One day, after the Devi Bhava ended, I stayed back waiting for another devotee. When Amma saw me, She came over and asked if there was any problem and why I was sitting there. As soon as Amma's mother saw Her talking to me, she came and started scolding Amma, using very harsh and cruel words. She pulled Amma roughly by the arm and took Her back into the house.

I felt terrible that it was because of me that Amma received such a severe scolding. I was deeply hurt and affected by the harsh words that were spoken against Her. After some time Amma returned to the temple. I hid behind a wall, as I did not want to create a problem for Amma again. Later I went to the temple and found Amma meditating as usual, as if nothing had happened. I, on the other hand, couldn't meditate for several days after that, because I was so affected by the way Amma's mother had treated Her. It was painful for me to see Amma being scolded like that. Even today, whenever I remember that incident, it brings tears to my eyes.

However, with regard to the behavior of Amma's parents, there is no sense in blaming them. Like any other parents, they wanted their daughters to get married. If any of the four daughters were not married, it would create a bad name for the family, and they were afraid of that. Also, at that time they did not know who Amma was. They didn't have the spiritual background to understand Amma. With the passing of time, their attitude changed. After reading books and talking with the devotees and the ashram residents, they slowly realized Amma's greatness. It was only because of their ignorance that they treated Her so badly during Her early life.

As I look back at that incident after the Devi Bhava, I realize the importance of remaining unaffected and detached from anything negative that happens to us. We can see an even-minded attitude in Amma. Praise or criticism doesn't affect Her, because She has insulated Her mind. She is always established in Her own Self.

Amma says, "Do not be satisfied with your ordinary state of worldly consciousness. There is a supreme state of blissfulness, an all-knowing and all-powerful state that can be attained by every one of you. Direct your mind and activities toward this end and strive to achieve the ultimate goal."

Everybody has a defective mind: some people have a lot of anger within; others have hatred, impatience, greed or jealousy. But we all have positive qualities as well. We should work hard to remove the negative traits and improve the positive qualities of our mind. This will make us truly happy and our lives will be a blessing for the world.

AS THE PERCEIVER, SO THE PERCEPTION

When we are disturbed by a negative emotion, we can try to replace it with a positive one. For example, when we feel hatred for someone, we can try to cultivate or nurture the feeling of love. Amma says that we should try to recall any good words spoken by that person, a good deed he or she has performed, or any help that person has offered us. Thus, we can slowly reduce the hatred in our mind. If we are angry toward somebody, we should try to kindle the feeling of compassion or kindness toward him or her. It may not be possible to go and hug that person and say, "I love you so much!" Nonetheless, at least mentally we can try to be forgiving and kind to that person. Whether we start today or tomorrow, it is imperative that we feel and express love and compassion if we really want to rid ourselves of the burden and restlessness created by negative feelings.

If we are sad and upset about some failure in our lives, we should try instead to think about some of our successes and be grateful to God for those. In this way, by exchanging positive emotions for negative ones, we can slowly reduce the strength of the negative feelings.

Suppose we are looking at a rose bush in bloom. There are two ways of looking at it. One way is to behold the beautiful flowers amidst the many thorns. That is the positive way of looking at it, forgetting the thorns totally and enjoying the flowers. Another way of looking at it is to focus on the number of thorns and be upset and angry at God for creating them among those beautiful flowers. It is our choice: we can either look at the flowers or focus on the thorns. Both exist; what we see depends on our outlook or perspective. Similarly, if we can look at the happy experiences in our lives, it will strengthen us; but if we look only at the painful experiences, we will become weak and depressed.

Everyone's life is a mixture of success and failure. So when we are successful, we can be grateful to God. If we fail, let us keep trying to be successful. And if we cannot achieve success despite our best efforts, then let us learn to accept the situation with a positive attitude. In the midst of all the mighty forces of nature, even though we may be weak, feeble and limited in terms of knowledge and capacity, we are able to survive. We are so small and insignificant in this enormous creation—an accident or death could occur anywhere at anytime. So each day when we wake up, we should be thankful to God. This is a positive way of looking at life. This life is a result of what we have done in the past. Therefore, by adjusting and correcting our lives in the present, we can always create a better future. This is why Amma says that we should try to live fully and positively in the present. If we think about past failures and worry about future problems, we cannot make good use of the present. Amma says, "The present is a present, presented to us by God. So use it well."

At one time, Swami Paramatmananda, another of Amma's senior disciples, had to undergo spinal surgery in the United States. Most disciples or devotees facing a major medical procedure would like to talk to Amma and get Her blessings. Certainly a few words from Amma at such a time give us tremendous strength and consolation. Swami Paramatmananda tried many times to talk to Amma over the phone but did not succeed. The matter was conveyed to Amma, and She then tried to contact him, but didn't succeed due to poor telephone connections. Then Amma left for a program in another city where the crowd was huge and She was so busy that She didn't have time to call him.

Swami Paramatmananda underwent the surgery, which went well. After a few days Amma called him and inquired about his health. Amma also asked him if he was angry at Her for not having called him. He replied, "No, Amma. I prayed to the Amma within me and felt so peaceful." Thus instead of feeling dejected that Amma did not call him, he drew courage and solace from Her presence within.

During such situations, if we do not receive personal attention or consolation from Amma, instead of being disconsolate we should try to draw courage and solace from Her inner presence. Situations such as these can help us to feel our Master's presence within us, and develop our strength and maturity. Depending on our approach and outlook, a situation may be viewed as either a stumbling block or a steppingstone.

THE SELFLESS LOVE OF A SATGURU

There are many people who claim to be Self-realized Gurus of the highest order. Generally, genuine Masters do not claim anything. Whom are we going to accept as our Guru? Surrender to a fake guru can cause chaos and confusion in our lives. Are there any guidelines that we can safely follow to make this important decision?

The unmistakable mark of a Satguru is the unconditional love and compassion He or She showers on everyone. A Satguru is never greedy for money, power or fame.

Most of us have experienced falling in love with another person. In contrast to this, in the presence of a genuine Master, we experience the beauty of what Amma calls *rising* in love. The magic touch of this divine love purifies and sanctifies every situation, every relationship, and every action in life. This experience opens up a new opportunity for us to learn how to love selflessly. It is very difficult to love an idea wholeheartedly, however lofty or noble it may be. After meeting Amma, pursuing the concept of selfless love comes more easily.

Human minds need a personal touch for the seeds of love to sprout. If anybody seeks love, attention and care, Amma is happy to help. The Guru is interested only in our welfare and growth, nothing else. She doesn't want anything in return.

When there is someone like Amma available to us, we can easily turn our hearts toward Her. At least let us try to love Amma without expecting anything. She is retaining

Her body selflessly only to offer us a tangible form for our selfless love.

Even though the Master is in the body, He or She represents the Truth beyond the body. Through the medium of a Master we behold the Truth, because the Master is a perfect representation of the Truth, selfless love and compassion.

If we have painful experiences after coming to a Guru, we can view those experiences as a way of removing or exhausting our past karma. Although Amma can take over or mitigate our karma, She says, "A certain percentage of our negative karma must be experienced by us."

Karma is the result of what we have done in the past. Everybody has to go through experiences brought about by their own karma. But with the Satguru's grace, our suffering can be reduced. If the bad karma cannot be mitigated, the Satguru can help by giving us the strength of mind we need to cope with the situation.

When we experience something painful, it is not that the Satguru did not help us; it is because of the nature of our negative karma. We should not find fault with the Guru. People are often heard saying, "See how many years I have prayed to the Guru! So, how can this happen to me?" We should look instead at all the benefits that have come to us because of the Guru. In this way, our faith can be reinforced.

By blaming or moving away from the Satguru, we may incur more pain and suffering. It is just like running away from a doctor in order to avoid the pain of an injection.

You may feel you have escaped from the pain when all you have done is deny the doctor the opportunity to save you from greater pain and suffering.

I would like to relate an experience of Swami Purnamritananda, another of Amma's senior disciples. This incident took place many years ago, soon after he met Amma. At that time Swami Purnamritananda (then Sreekumar) was still living with his parents, but he would stay at the ashram day and night without returning home. He was the only son of his parents, and they were not happy with the situation and often tried to discourage him from returning to the ashram. As he was adamant about spending most of his time there, they compromised, agreeing that he could spend his days with Amma but that he would have to return home every night. After that, he would visit the ashram daily, but he used to leave after the evening bhajans in order to appease his parents.

One night as he was preparing to leave, Amma told him that he should stay at the ashram that night. Swami Purnamritananda told Amma that if he spent the night, his parents would surely not let him return to the ashram the next day. But Amma insisted. Not wanting to disobey Her, he agreed to stay.

Later that night after dinner, Swami Purnamritananda was walking back and forth near the little temple, chanting his mantra. He heard a rustling in the grass at his feet and stopped to investigate the source of the sound. Suddenly he felt a painful stab in his foot. Scanning the ground he saw the outline of a snake as it slithered into the darkness.

He cried out in pain and shock. Amma immediately jumped up from where She had been seated inside the temple with some of the other brahmacharis and rushed to his side. He was speechless and could only show Amma the wound on his foot. Without hesitation, Amma bent down and put Her mouth to the wound, sucking the poison out and spitting on the ground. After repeating this process several times, She tied a cloth over the wound. As Swami Purnamritananda was still a bit shaken, She sent him to see a local traditional healer, who was known for his ability to treat snakebites.

The healer examined Swami Purnamritananda and told him that he had been bitten by an extremely poisonous snake, but that the poison seemed to be gone and that he would be all right. The healer then gave him some medicinal herbs and sent him away.

Later that night, Amma told Swami Purnamritananda that he was going through a bad time astrologically. Because She knew that his parents would not believe it simply because She said so, She suggested that he consult an astrologer.

The next morning, he returned to his family. His parents were angry with him for not having returned the previous night. He asked them to hear him out and showed them the wound on his foot. But they only said that if he had kept his promise and had returned home the previous night, he would not have been bitten by a snake.

Swami Purnamritananda also informed his parents about what Amma had said regarding his astrological chart.

They agreed that a snakebite was a bad omen, and a few days later they took him to see an astrologer. Upon consulting Swami Purnamritananda's chart, the astrologer was surprised to see that his client was still alive! According to his chart, the astrologer said that wherever he might have been that night, he was destined to receive a fatal snakebite. "You are definitely under divine protection," the astrologer said.

"See," said Swami Purnamritananda to his parents, "you said it was only because I stayed with Amma that night that I was bitten by a snake. But, in fact, I would have received a snakebite that night wherever I happened to be. If I had been at home, would you have sucked the poison out of my wound the way Amma did? And our home is in a remote place; I wouldn't have been able to reach a hospital in time. Had I disobeyed Amma and returned home that night, I would have died."

The nature of some karma is such that it has to be experienced in a human body. If Amma removes such karma from another person, She has to experience it Herself. Amma says that if She takes a serious illness from someone, She can exhaust that karma in a few minutes, whereas that person would otherwise have had to suffer for many years.

One of the brahmacharis, who was well qualified and had a good job, was totally transformed after meeting Amma. Within a few days he left his job and joined the ashram. Amma warned him that he could expect a lot of problems from his family.

His parents and relatives tried in every way to get him to leave the ashram. They even tried to kidnap him. But they failed in their attempts. Finally, they resorted to black magic. It was powerful enough to make the brahmachari severely sick and even kill him. Nobody knew about this until Amma told us several months later.

Suddenly, Amma caught a cough. The cough became worse, and after a few days She was coughing continuously. Yet, amazingly, during the Devi Bhava darshan the cough would stop. Then, as soon as the Devi Bhava was over, She would resume coughing intensely. We tried to persuade Her to visit a doctor, but She refused. All the brahmacharis were terribly upset. Many of them started fasting as a penance for the sake of Amma's health. When Amma learned about this, She told us to stop fasting, but we didn't stop. We said that we wanted to fast until She was cured. Amma then told us that Her health would be restored in one week, whether or not we fasted or even if She went to a doctor, because Her cough was not the result of an infection or any illness but was due to the effect of black magic.

As Amma predicted, exactly one week later Her cough suddenly disappeared, and She regained Her health. She told us then that if She had not taken the effects of that black magic upon Herself, it would have killed the person against whom it was intended. Thus, out of Her compassion, She took upon Herself the effects of that terrible deed.

THE SIGNIFICANCE
OF SPIRITUAL PRACTICES

If we are committed to attaining the goal of spirituality, we have to realize that the spiritual path is not lined with roses. Indeed, the path is difficult, but the hurdles should not be an excuse to give up our spiritual practices. Think of the fullness and perfection that can be achieved by attaining the final goal of union with the Supreme, the state of Yoga.

Sometimes, we may want to compromise our meditation and other spiritual practices. There is often something "more important" that must be done instead. Meditation and other spiritual practices are on our daily list of things to do, but these items get pushed down to the bottom of the list of priorities. We may be able to justify our decision, thinking that meditation and other spiritual practices can always be done tomorrow. Inconsistency in our spiritual practice is one of the reasons we are not able to make any steady progress on the spiritual path.

Our spiritual quest has to be sincere, for only then will there be any real results. We should be aware of the necessity and urgency of our spiritual practices.

Many people are very busy, but they somehow find an hour or two to walk or do some exercise every day on the advice of their doctor. They know that if they don't, they will have serious health problems. However busy these people are, they will not neglect their exercise.

Likewise, meditation should become an important part of our lives. Amma always says that meditation, *japa* (repetition of a mantra) and other spiritual practices are as valuable as gold. These practices give us spiritual growth as well as material prosperity. They also help us to maintain our mental and emotional health. Therefore, the time we spend in meditation and other spiritual practices will never be a waste.

THE FIFTY-FIFTY APPROACH

We may spend one whole day listening to discourses about God and thinking only about God. Tomorrow, we may think it's all right if we don't meditate but instead watch TV the whole day, because the whole of yesterday we were thinking of God. If we spend one day like this, and another day like that, then we won't make any real progress. If we want to have the full benefit, Amma says, "Whatever you do, whatever you say, whatever you think—all these things should prepare you for meditation." Otherwise, it is like taking ten steps forward and then slipping back ten steps.

There is a saying that half of what we achieve is accomplished by our effort and the rest by God's grace. Some people say, "I am content with half success. So, let God give me His share first. I can just sit back and relax." Amma says that a fifty-fifty approach like that will not give us the full benefit. Water boils at 100 degrees centigrade. But that does not mean that at 50 degrees, 50% of the water will boil!

Once a man on a business trip got stuck in a small town mid-way through his journey. That night he stayed in a motel. As he had been traveling for two or three weeks, he missed his wife, children, and especially the delicious chicken curry his wife often prepared. He was thinking, "Oh, how nice it would be to have some chicken curry just the way my wife makes it!" As he continued thinking about it, the desire to have chicken curry became over-whelming. He looked in the telephone directory. To his pleasant surprise, he found that there was a restaurant just a few blocks away that served chicken curry. Since it was already late, he didn't want to take a chance, so he took a taxi to the restaurant. There on the menu he saw the exact dish he had been thinking about. No sooner had he ordered that dish than the waiter served it. He was surprised by the size of the serving. For such a reasonable price, the dish was brimful with pieces of chicken breast. He thought, "Oh, I must tell all my friends to come and eat here!" But as he started eating he thought, "They gave me so much chicken, but none of it tastes like chicken. It tastes like steak." He called the waiter and asked him, "What's in this dish?"

"Just chicken breast, nothing else," the waiter replied.

The man was not satisfied with the answer. He rushed to the manager and said in a raised voice, "I asked for chicken curry, but I have been given something else. Not a single piece tastes like chicken!"

"No, sir. It is definitely chicken. There is nothing else in that dish," the manager said.

"I don't believe it," the businessman exclaimed. "I'm going to complain to the authorities!"

Then the manager said in a low voice, "Sir, if you have any complaints, I will refund your money. The truth is that we ran out of chicken today, so we added a little steak to the chicken curry."

"Only a little! All the pieces tasted like steak. How much steak did you add to the chicken?"

"Only fifty-fifty, sir."

"Fifty-fifty? I don't believe it! Do you mean to say you added steak to chicken by equal weight?"

"Not exactly, sir. By fifty-fifty, I mean one chicken for one cow!"

No wonder the businessman couldn't find any chicken on his plate!

We may spend one day in an ashram, and then spend our time the next day in a casino. Because of our lack of receptivity, even if we spend one full day at the ashram, the effect may be minimal. In contrast, due to our strong vasanas, if we spend one day in a casino, the effect may be very strong. In such a situation, whatever benefit we get from doing spiritual practices will not be fully realized, just as the taste of one chicken will be overwhelmed by the taste of one cow.

To get the maximum benefit from spiritual practices, Amma says it is important for all of us to cultivate some sort of discipline in our lives: fasting, keeping a vow of silence for specific hours or days, doing more meditation, spending more time chanting a mantra, reading spiritual books, etc. Spiritual discipline can take any form, depending on what suits us.

CHAPTER 7

PREPARATION FOR MEDITATION

AUM SHANTI, SHANTI, SHANTI

S hanti means peace. Very often, auspicious events conclude with the mantra, "Aum shanti, shanti, shanti." Disturbances to our peace come from three sources, which is why we chant "peace" three times.

1) Disturbances that come from natural forces (*adhi daivikam*). Earthquakes, cyclones, floods, droughts, heat and cold belong to this group. Can we meditate peacefully in the middle of an earthquake or when floodwater is inundating our house? We have no control over such things. We can only run to safety and pray for peace from these natural forces. This is why we chant the first "shanti."

2) Disturbances we experience from the world around us (*adhi bhautikam*). If our neighbor's son is playing pop or disco music loudly or their dog is barking when we are trying to meditate, it will be a hindrance to our meditation. Mosquitoes, flies, and vehicles on the road are all examples of such disturbances. Some of them can be taken care of, as they are partially under our control. For example, if our neighbor's son is too troublesome, we can talk to him and his parents. If that doesn't work, we can call the police. Or if mosquitoes are bothering us when we are trying to

meditate, we can sit inside a mosquito net or burn a mosquito coil to get rid of the mosquitoes.

3) Disturbances that come from within (*adhyatmikam*). These are our likes and dislikes, anger, jealousy, restlessness, agitation, etc. All of us suffer from these internal disturbances. Even though at present we are at their mercy, with proper spiritual practice they can be brought totally under our control. If we are alert and able to use our discrimination, we can control all the negative tendencies of the mind. The disturbances that come from within are the most powerful disturbances of all, more powerful than an earthquake or a cyclone, because they can totally destroy our peace and our happiness. Fortunately, this third type of disturbance can be completely eliminated, unlike the first two types of disturbances.

Amma once told the following story. There was a man who wanted to be in an atmosphere that was perfect for his meditation. He tried many different places. Wherever he went, there was some sort of disturbance—the birds were chirping, dogs were barking, or people were fighting and yelling. So he thought, "I want a room that is soundproof." He then sat inside a soundproof room and started meditating. As we all know, when there is absolute silence, even a small sound will be experienced as a loud noise. When he meditated in his soundproof room, even the ticking of his watch disturbed him. The noise seemed so loud that he finally threw the watch away. He then resumed his meditation. After some time, he began to hear his own heartbeat. When the watch made too much noise, he threw away the watch, but how could he throw away his heart?

Amma says that total freedom from external disturbances is not possible because the world isn't dead—it's alive. There is so much activity in the world that there will always be some noise and disturbances. If there were no disturbances at all when we tried to meditate, we would probably fall asleep. It's quite easy for most of us to fall asleep when there are no disturbances. Many of us have no trouble sleeping even amidst loud noises. I have even witnessed people sleeping in the same room where loud bhajans were being sung!

In the early years, when the ashram was very small, there was only a small temple and two or three huts where we lived. Backwaters surrounded the ashram. Near the ashram there were a few places where the local people made coir rope out of coconut fiber.

The coconut fiber (the external green fiber) is soaked in the backwaters for several days, after which it is taken out and beaten with a stick until each fiber is separated. Rope is made by twisting these fibers together.

From seven o'clock in the morning onward we could hear the sound of 300 women beating the coconut fibers with sticks while talking loudly! It was such a disturbance. And that was the time when our meditation session began each morning with Amma sitting amongst us. It was good training for all of us in striving to overcome external disturbances.

Amma used to say, "It is easy to meditate in the mountain caves of the Himalayas. There is no one to disturb us. If we can get the same deep meditation in the midst of a market, then it can be said that we have mastered the art of meditation."

A pure mind is the most important factor in meditation. Once the mind becomes pure and mature, there will no longer be any disturbances. Then meditation becomes spontaneous.

QUIETING INTERNAL DISTURBANCES

Initially it is necessary to make some mental adjustments before trying to dive deep into meditation. There are bound to be external or internal disturbances. Whatever these disturbances may be, we won't be able to meditate or do any other spiritual practices without some adjustment. Having adjusted to the external disturbances to a certain extent, we can focus on our own internal disturbances, which, as mentioned earlier, include our likes and dislikes, anger, impatience, etc. Even if the external situation is very calm and quiet, disturbances in our mind will compromise our meditation.

One day I was standing in front of the little temple at the ashram. Some incense sticks were burning, and a pleasant fragrance pervaded the air. A devotee came up and asked me where we had purchased the wonderful incense. I replied that we made it ourselves at the ashram. The devotee talked with me for a while, and then he went inside the temple to meditate. People like to meditate inside that temple because Amma used to give Devi Bhava darshan there in the early days. Because of this, the spiritual vibrations inside are very powerful. Concentration is easier for those who are able to attune to those vibrations.

When I went into the temple a little later, I saw this same person meditating, sitting with his spine straight, eyes closed—a perfect posture. After some time, as he was leaving the temple I asked him if he'd had a good meditation. "No, Swami!' he said. "As soon as I sat down and closed my eyes, I began thinking about the incense. Last week I went to a shop and bought some incense, but it wasn't of a good quality at all, and the shopkeeper charged me too much for it. When I was trying to meditate, I kept thinking about this, and I felt very angry with the shopkeeper. In my mind I was fighting with him the whole time."

So, even though this man was sitting in the temple, a place filled with Amma's divine vibrations, he could not meditate even for a short time. All that he could do was fight mentally with the shopkeeper!

Even if we find ourselves in the most suitable atmosphere, if our mind is distracted, we cannot meditate peacefully. That is why it's more important to work on the internal disturbances than the external ones. Amma says that we may be sitting in an excellent posture, while inside we are waging a great war, boiling with anger, frustration or hatred.

INTEGRATION OF THE INNER
AND OUTER WORLD

Since it is a cumbersome process to remove our negative tendencies, we compromise and live with them. Sometimes we conceal such feelings and behave well outwardly. Suppose we happen to meet someone whom we don't like at all. Even so, we may say, "I'm so happy to see you!" We may dislike that person, but we don't tell him or her that. We hide it because that is considered good manners. On occasion, we may have been standing in a long line at the supermarket, having to wait for ten to fifteen minutes. Just when we begin to lose our patience, the cashier answers the telephone and then explains she must step away from the checkout line for a few minutes, but that she will be right back. We are getting more and more impatient. Finally she returns saying, "I'm so sorry! I had to attend to an urgent call."

Even though we feel extremely impatient, we'll say, "It's okay. Take your time." These are normal, decent manners. In a way, it's good that we are able to hide or control our negative feelings and present a positive image on the outside. We may have a friend who is ugly, but even so, we'd never say to him or her, "Hey, you are really an ugly duckling!" If that friend happens to ask, "How do I look?" we will say, "You look fine," or we may even say, "You look handsome."

It is appropriate to be polite to others outwardly even though we may feel different internally, but while meditating we have to be totally integrated. When we meditate, we are face to face with our own mind; we cannot hide from or lie to ourselves. Because of this, as much attention should be given to correcting the negativity of the mind as to the technique of meditation. Unless the mind is relatively calm and quiet, it is impossible to meditate. This doesn't mean that we have to wait to meditate until we become relatively calm; that would create a tendency in us to postpone our meditation practice. If we think, "Right now I am agitated and restless, so I'll wait until I'm calm and after that I'll start to meditate," it's never going to happen. We need to meditate and to work on our negativity simultaneously. Amma gives a metaphor: "To think that you will start meditating only when you are totally calm and at peace is like standing on the shore waiting for all the waves to subside so that you can start swimming. That's impossible."

Once when Amma was on Her yearly North Indian tour, She paid a visit to the sacred city of Haridwar, through which the holy river Ganges flows. While She was in Haridwar, Amma went to the Ganges to bathe. The water was so cold that we couldn't even put our feet in the water. Around us people were making a lot of noise— blowing conches, chanting mantras, children were screaming and shouting, and vendors were hawking their wares. Amma was just gazing at the flowing river. All of a sudden She got into the freezing water. Within minutes, Amma was in samadhi. The noise, the ice-cold water and other external distractions didn't affect Her at all. Holding onto a pole because of the power of the rushing current, She stood, waist-deep in the water, completely lost to the world for a couple of hours. We finally had to carry Her out; otherwise She would have continued to stand in the freezing water for any number of hours. As She was being carried out of the water, Her body was as stiff as a board. The brahmacharinis rubbed Her hands and the soles of Her feet. After about half an hour, Her body regained some heat, and She returned to normal consciousness.

Once the mind attains a sublime state, no external disturbance is a problem. We see this state reflected in Amma. For Her to be affected by anything, She has to allow Herself to be affected.

TRAINING THE MIND TO STAY IN THE PRESENT

I remember an incident that took place in Sweden a few years ago. On the last evening of the European tour, there was no program and the group traveling with Amma had a chance to be alone with Her. Amma served dinner to everybody, joked with us and told us stories. It was the most memorable occasion of the three-month tour. There was one hard-working devotee who was sitting right next to Amma. Amma was stroking her hair and back lovingly, showering her with affection. It must have been a wonderful experience for that person. The other group members were feeling a bit envious. After a few minutes, the woman started sobbing. We all thought she was overwhelmed by

Amma's love and affection. Amma asked her, "Darling daughter, why are you crying?" She replied that she was crying because that morning Amma had called everybody for meditation, but she had not been informed about it. Amma said, "Why are you thinking about what happened this morning? That has become the past. Right now you are sitting close to Amma. No one else has this chance now. So try to make the best use of this opportunity. Instead of brooding over the past and making yourself miserable, enjoy the present situation."

This is how we waste many of our opportunities. Amma always says that we should try to live in the present moment. If we live in the past, we cannot possibly enjoy what is happening right now. Life is always in the present. Training the mind to stay in the present moment is real meditation.

ATTITUDE AND ACTION

The right attitude helps in meditation also. The impact of all of our actions and thoughts can be felt when we sit for meditation. Every thought, every action, each emotion determines the quality of our meditation. So we must be careful not to engage in activities that will serve as a hindrance to our meditation. We perform many actions in our day-to-day life that are not really necessary. Such actions can gradually be avoided, though it may not be possible to stop them immediately.

Suppose we are in the habit of watching horror movies or reading murder mysteries. It will be good if we can avoid such anxiety-inducing activities because those thoughts will remain in our subconscious mind. During our meditation all these memories will resurface. Through proper understanding, slowly we can avoid such actions and replace them with good actions that will be helpful to our spiritual growth.

In the early days, there were fewer devotees, and Amma had not yet started any institutions or organized charitable activities. Amma devoted a great deal of time each day to being with the devotees who visited the ashram. She talked to them, answered their questions, cleared their doubts, and gave them a lot of personal attention and care. This gave them the precious opportunity to feel close to Her. One day a new devotee came to see Amma. He didn't know much about Her, but he stayed in the ashram for a week.

The whole week he saw Amma spending most of Her time with the devotees, with not much sleep or food for Herself. Finally, he asked, "Amma, you are asking the brahmacharis to meditate, but I never see you meditate. Why?"

Amma replied, "Whatever I do is meditation. When I am giving darshan or spending time with the devotees, I always see them as God."

Some of you may have heard Amma chanting, "Amma, Amma," while receiving devotees. So, if there are 1000 people for darshan, She will chant the mantra at least 1000 times. In India thousands of people come to Her for darshan each day. Thus, Amma is converting even Her darshan into an act of worship. Of course, there is no need for Amma to chant mantras or to meditate, because She is already established in God-consciousness. Amma is doing these things to teach us a lesson and to be a role model for us.

Amma sees even ordinary human beings as God, whereas we are not able to see the Goddess (Amma) as the Goddess, even after having many powerful experiences with Her. We forget the truth that Amma is the Goddess. Though many of us know in our heart of hearts that Amma is the Divine Mother, how often do we remember this? Many times we consider Her to be just like a friend! I have heard some people addressing Amma, "Hi, how are you?" On one occasion, I heard someone asking Amma, "When do 'you guys' sleep?" In spite of Amma manifesting all the divine qualities, we tend to be casual in what we say to Her and how we say it.

We may worship Amma, prostrate to Amma, or do puja to Amma. Unfortunately, even while we are doing all these things, our mind wanders away. In contrast, Amma, in spite of all our shortcomings and vices, constantly sees us as God. For such a being, no other meditation is necessary.

CHAPTER 8

THE PATH OF DEVOTION

FOUR TYPES OF DEVOTEES

Hinduism, otherwise known as *Sanatana Dharma* (The Eternal Way of Life), has set forth various paths for Self-realization. These many paths are intended for seekers of different intellectual and mental dispositions. None of these paths can be considered higher or lower than any other. Lord Krishna corroborates this fact in the 12th chapter of the *Bhagavad Gita*, entitled *Bhakti Yoga* (Yoga of Devotion). In this chapter, Arjuna asks Krishna, "O Lord, there are devotees who love and worship Thee as a Divine Person and again there are others who contemplate Thee as formless power. Which of these paths is supreme?" In His answer Krishna implies that both paths are equally meritorious and the suitability of each path depends on the qualities of the seeker. A baby requires soft and easily digestible food whereas a grownup may require food with a higher caloric value. Likewise, different paths are fitting for different seekers.

There are very few people who feel pure love for God. Most people pray to God that they be saved from sorrows or for the fulfillment of their needs and desires. Accordingly, devotees have been classified in the *Bhagavad Gita* into four groups.

1) People undergoing suffering (*artta*)

2) People who seek riches or fulfillment of desires (*artharthi*)

3) People in search of God (*jijnasu*)

4) People who have found and become established in God (*jnani*)

People in distress become devotees in order to find relief from sorrow and to have their grievances removed. Once their sorrows have been dispelled, they stop praying or worshipping God until the next time they find themselves in distress. For them, God is like an agent to do their work and to fulfill their desires. They usually fail to realize that their attachment to impermanent worldly objects is the cause of their sorrow. God, for them, is like a painkiller tablet. That sort of devotion treats only the symptoms when they appear. The cause of disease is not removed.

People in the second category are those who have many worldly desires, who are often greedy and ambitious and who seek God's help for the fulfillment of their desires. Such people may already be quite comfortably well off, but they are not content. They love God mainly because God can fulfill their cherished desires. They give donations to charities or to a church or temple with the attitude of someone paying an insurance premium or making a business investment, expecting a handsome return.

A jijnasu is a person who has reached a state of disillusionment with the world and all worldly enjoyments. The futility of all worldly goals has been impressed upon him or her, and this devotee seeks to know the higher truths of life. Such a person prays to God for devotion, dispassion and true knowledge and wisdom, which alone can grant true happiness.

A jnani is one who is totally identified with God. Such a person sees God in everything and is never distracted from unbroken meditation on the Ultimate Truth. Though complete and perfect in every respect, a jnani retains a devotee's nature just to enjoy God's *lila* (divine play). Love for God is a natural state for the jnani. Of all the devotees, the jnani is dearest to the Lord. Krishna says, "The jnani is My very Self." In the *Srimad Bhagavatam*, the Lord admits, "I am a slave of My devotees. My heart is in the grip of My devotee, for such is My love for him or her." God will go to any extent to protect those devoted to Him.

There are significant differences among these four types of devotees. In the *Bhagavad Gita*, Krishna declares that all devotees are noble (*udarah*). Even the artta and artharthi are trying to find real and lasting happiness, albeit through worldly attainments. In due course, these seekers slowly overcome all worldly attachments and come to realize that to attain real and lasting happiness, one has to realize the Eternal Reality, i.e., God or the Atman. Their devotion becomes more and more pure, and slowly they evolve to become jijnasus (seekers of the Truth or God) and later jnanis. Krishna declared that anyone who is devoted to Him should be deemed righteous, for such a person has taken the right resolve and soon attains lasting peace. For some, this transformation can come within one lifetime; for others, it may take many births. Sooner or later, everyone will attain the Supreme.

QUALITIES OF A TRUE DEVOTEE

In the epic *Srimad Bhagavatam*, the Lord says that He follows the footsteps of His devotees in order to wear the dust of their feet on His forehead. If the Lord becomes such a loving servant of someone, then that person is indeed a true devotee. Who, then, is a true devotee? Krishna explains the qualities of a true devotee in the *Bhagavad Gita* (Chapter XII, Verses 13-16).

The Lord says that the first quality of a true devotee is that he or she has no hatred for any being in this entire creation. We feel hatred when something or someone comes in the way of our having our desires, enjoyments and expectations fulfilled. We expect many things from others, and when our expectations are not fulfilled, we begin to dislike or hate those people. Only love that is free from expectations is true love. A true devotee has no expectations of anyone. Such a devotee has equal vision toward all. He or she accepts whatever comes, good or bad, as God's sweet will.

Another cause for developing hatred for somebody is the feeling that the other person is different from oneself. Jnanis see themselves in all of creation, and they see all of creation in themselves. They are full of love for all beings in the world. This love for all beings is the second quality of a true devotee.

The best example of this is Amma, who says, "An unbroken stream of Love flows from Me toward all beings in the cosmos." Amma feels no hatred or even resentment toward any being in this universe. "Those who hate Me and those who love Me are the same to Me," says Amma. She has equal love for all. Her love encompasses the entire Creation.

Amma explains universal love with a beautiful example. "If our hand accidentally pokes our eye, we do not punish our hand or blame our eye, because they are parts of our own body. So, too, the same Consciousness pervades the whole universe, and the whole Creation is the embodiment of God." A true devotee sees his or her beloved God in all beings. So, there is no place in his or her heart for any negative feelings toward others.

Many years ago, after Amma's cousin had tried to kill Amma, he was admitted to the hospital with a fatal illness. Before he died, Amma visited him at the hospital. She caressed and consoled him and lovingly fed him food with Her own hands. The cousin was filled with remorse for what he had tried to do, and he burst into tears, having experienced for himself Amma's compassion and forgiveness.

A striking incident in the life of Saint Namadev illustrates the universal love of a true devotee. Namadev was an ardent devotee of the Lord and had reached the great heights of God-realization. One day Namadev was going to eat his lunch, which consisted of a few chapattis (dry, flat bread) and a little butter. As he was about to eat, a stray dog came in and ran off with a chapatti. Namadev ran after the dog with the rest of the chapattis in his hand. After a long chase, he finally caught up with the dog. He took the chapatti from the dog's mouth and started spreading butter on it, entreating the dog with love and devotion, "O Lord, do not eat these dry chapattis. They may get stuck in your throat. Please have some butter with them." Namadev was seeing the dog as a manifestation of the Lord. By feeding the dog, he was feeding the Lord Himself. Such is the marvelous vision of a true devotee.

For true devotees, God is their All in all. They see everything as God's will and accept everything—good or bad, pleasant or unpleasant—as God's prasad. The true devotee's devotion is steady in all circumstances. He or she does not grumble nor feel dissatisfied even when placed in unfavorable circumstances. God dwells in the heart of a true devotee and rushes to help him or her whenever there is trouble. If the call of a devotee is sincere, God will respond immediately. The more intense the prayer of a devotee, the quicker will be God's response.

Neelambaran is an ardent devotee of Amma. He stays in a village near the ashram. He was a farm laborer and would unfailingly come for Amma's bhava darshans after his day's work in the fields. A few years ago he faced some financial problems. One day while working in the fields, he unwittingly said, "As I have no money, I think my family will have to starve in the coming days."

His co-workers often criticized Amma. Having heard what he said, they made fun of Neelambaran saying, "Why are you worried? Surely, the young girl whom you address and worship as Devi will bring you the money!" On hearing their mocking words, Neelambaran felt very sad and prayed earnestly to Amma to help him out of this tight situation. The lunch break arrived, and as the workers sat in the shade of a tree, a girl suddenly approached Neelambaran with a twenty-rupee note in her hand. Without uttering a word, she placed it in Neelambaran's hand and left immediately. Neelambaran was taken aback as he had never seen this girl before. He didn't know why she had placed the twenty-rupee note in his hand. The other workers thought the girl was repaying some debt, but Neelambaran hadn't lent money to anyone. The workers asked Neelambaran who the girl was. He said he didn't know. The workers were also surprised.

During Devi Bhava the next day, when Neelambaran went for Amma's darshan, She uttered in his ear, "Son, did Devi give you money yesterday? My child, it was Amma that came to you." Neelambaran was awestruck and tears of devotion streamed down his cheeks.

A true devotee surrenders everything—his or her body, mind, and intellect—to God, and depends on God entirely. Such surrender is difficult to achieve. When trying situations arise, we may give up this spirit of surrender. Many people claim to have taken refuge in God, yet they tend to forget this; they believe only in their own powers. They take pride in their own abilities to solve problems.

When the ego comes into play, all surrender vanishes. There is a story of Lord Shiva which clearly reveals this truth.

One day Lord Shiva was sitting with His holy consort, Parvati, on Mount Kailas. He suddenly got up and went out without uttering a word. Parvati was surprised. However, after just a few seconds, Lord Shiva returned and took his seat. Then Parvati asked, "My Lord, where did you go so hastily and why are you back so soon?"

The Lord said, "One of My devotees was being harassed by some troublemakers, and the devotee was praying to Me for help."

"Did you save him?" Parvati inquired.

Lord Shiva smiled and said, "There was no need of My intervention. As soon as I arrived there, I saw that he had taken a stone in his hand and at the same time was asking the local people to join him in the fight. So, I returned. If the devotee feels he can protect himself, what need is there for Me to come to his rescue?"

The significance of the story is not that we shouldn't defend ourselves if we are attacked or threatened. But we should always remember that it is God's power and not our own power or that of our fellow beings that brings victory.

EVERYTHING IS GOD'S WILL

A seeker following the path of devotion contemplates, "Everything is my Beloved. I am absolutely nothing. Everything takes place according to God's will."

The devotee considers him- or herself as an instrument of God or as God's servant, and hence the chances of becoming egoistic are less than for a seeker following another path. For a true devotee, everything is God. This is in stark contrast to a seeker on the path of knowledge, who thinks, "I am everything (the Self)."

The advantages of being a devotee are many. A true devotee's life is totally dedicated to God whatever the situation may be. Sorrows do not touch him or her. The devotee leads a carefree life under God's protective wing, always reveling in the thought of his or her beloved Lord. Yet such devotees are rare. To realize such pure devotion is like winning a lottery. The number of aspirants is so great and the winners are so few! It truly requires the supreme grace of God for someone to attain pure devotion. However, it is much easier for us, who have Amma in our midst as the very embodiment of divine love and grace.

The fruit of devotion can be enjoyed right from the beginning. As Amma puts it, "*Bhakti* (devotion) is like a jackfruit tree that bears fruit at the very base; the fruits can easily be plucked. In the case of other trees (which may be compared to other spiritual paths), you may have to climb high to pluck the fruit. On the path of devotion, you can enjoy the fruit of bliss right from the beginning, whereas on other paths it can be attained only at the end."

CHAPTER 9

THE PATH OF ACTION

UNDERSTANDING AND ACCEPTANCE WITH DETACHMENT

Why do we pray to God? Most of us pray because we want to be happy and contented. Simply stated, we pray to God to get something or to get rid of something. Suppose we have spent all our time in remembrance of our Guru or God, and yet we are besieged with troubles, one after the other. How long will our faith and devotion last? Who can go on loving an unseen God who never misses an opportunity to send us troubles and tribulations? In such circumstances one might even become an atheist. It would be even more difficult to love those who are instrumental in causing us pain and grief.

But look at Amma. She never received anyone's love during Her childhood. Her entire family and the villagers frequently scolded and ridiculed Her. There was nobody to strengthen Her soul with timely spiritual advice—no Guru. (Of course She did not really need a Master, as She was born with supreme knowledge and wisdom.) Despite all these adverse circumstances, She never complained, and not even once did She lose Her faith. For every bit of harsh treatment She received, She returned only love and compassion.

Amma has always been like the rose bush, which, receiving only cow dung and dirt, gives beauty and fragrance to the world.

I once asked Her, "Amma, didn't you feel disappointed with Your life, especially during that long period of hardship?"

Amma answered, "I was not at all disappointed, because I know the nature of people and of the world, and I never expect anything from anybody. I just go on doing My work and discharging My responsibilities without expecting anything. Hence, there is no disappointment." Amma also added that She doesn't wait to enjoy the results of Her actions but enjoys the very action itself. This is an important message for all of us.

We may think that Amma's caliber, courage and compassion are beyond our reach. Nevertheless, if we try to inculcate these teachings of Amma's, we can, without question, enhance our own lives.

For every circumstance we go through, there can be many possible outcomes. Unfortunately, due to our limited vision, we expect only one result and are disappointed if the result is different from what we anticipated. This is not to say that we simply have to accept everything the way it happens. One need not be a mere puppet in the hands of events. Let us try our best to get the result we want; but if that isn't possible, then we should learn to accept the outcome, whatever it is.

Sometimes, a situation will be such that we cannot run away from a problem—it is like trying to run away from our own feet! But at the same time, we might not have the strength to face the problem. What can we do?

What is needed is a clear understanding and acceptance of the situation. A man said to his friend, "On a cold day I know what to do—try to keep warm. If that isn't possible, then I know what else to do—freeze!"

The key to success in life, according to the Hindu scriptures, is to act wholeheartedly, without being attached to the fruits of that action, without being too concerned about the result. We may think it is impossible to act without expectation. Well, then, if expect you must, expect every possible outcome. Otherwise, be prepared for disappointment.

Suppose I need $1000, and I ask a friend to lend me that amount. There are five possible results.

1) He may give me $1000.

2) He may think I am a nice person and remember that I have helped him on many occasions. So he may give me more than $1000.

3) He, too, may have some financial difficulties and may only give me $500.

4) He may be having such financial difficulties that he won't be able to give me any money.

5) His financial difficulties may be even greater than mine, and instead of helping me, he may try to borrow some money from me. So I might end up lending him some money.

Thus I may get more than I asked for, or less than I asked for; I may get the exact amount I wanted, or I may not get anything at all. And I may even end up giving him some money, as his needs may be greater than mine. Any one of these outcomes is possible. We have no control over what could happen. As the *Bhagavad Gita* says, "We have the freedom to act, but not to determine the result, because the result of an action also depends on other factors. Hence, perform your actions without being attached to the results."

Recognizing this truth is not pessimism; it is simply being realistic. You may be familiar with Murphy's Law, which says, "Anything that can go wrong, will go wrong." For example, if a car can break down, it will break down. We can turn pessimism into realism by adding, "If it did not break down, be thankful to God." Only a strong and receptive mind can assimilate these truths.

EXERCISING THE MIND

Cultivating the strength and understanding to accept the results of our actions, whatever they may be, is real maturity. That is why Amma says mental and emotional maturity is very important for a happy and peaceful life.

Amma gives an example: If we exercise only the upper portions of our body, such as our arms and chest, those parts will undoubtedly develop strong muscles, while the lower parts of the body will be less developed. How funny a person will look with a muscular chest, biceps, and triceps, but with thin and weak thigh and calf muscles! The development will be disproportionate.

Most of us are physically strong and mature. Many people do physical exercises to keep themselves fit. Unfortunately, hardly anyone exercises the mind to make it strong and mature. If you want to become a good weightlifter, you have to practice lifting heavy weights. It is not enough to keep lifting a sheet of paper or a pencil. Similarly, if we want to be fully developed, we must exercise our mind, which is the basis for all our actions, words and thoughts. Difficult and challenging situations in life can be used as exercises for the mind.

When we act with too much attachment toward, or concern about, the result of an action, our performance becomes affected. When we take part in a competition, we naturally want to win the first prize, but many times our strong desire to win the prize can unsettle us. If we think more about winning than performing, the pressure to win will drain away our power. The mind cannot function well if it is attached to a result.

Let us take the example of a shooting competition. During the practice session many participants will perform exceedingly well. They are not thinking of shooting for any particular prize; they are just practicing. However, when they begin shooting in the real competition, they will be thinking of winning the prize and may become nervous. They might see two targets and miss the bull's eye! What has happened is not that the shooter's skills have diminished but that the thought of winning the prize has divided the person's attention, thus disturbing his or her concentration. I would like to relate one of my experiences in this regard.

After graduating from college, I applied for a job and was called for an interview. It was my first interview, and the pressure created by my resolve to land that particular job created a great deal of stress and tension in me. I was focused only on getting the job and on my concern about what to do if I didn't get it. As requested, I appeared for the interview. The interviewing officers asked only simple questions, but due to my state of mind at that time, I made a mess of the answers. My responses were anything but impressive. At the end of the interview, the chief officer said, "Thank you. We will let you know." That was years ago, and they still have not let me know anything!

Thus our obsession or anxiety about the results of our actions takes its toll on us. Amma always says that while performing, you should focus your full attention on the performance; do not even think about the result. Before starting your performance, be sure about your goal. But, while performing, there shouldn't be any disturbance or distraction in your mind.

Amma gained amazing psychological maturity at a very young age, and She did this by learning from every adverse situation She had to face. Every difficult experience was a passage from the book of life, which She assimilated without any grudge or hatred toward anyone. Her alertness, awareness and discrimination made Her capable of digesting all types of experiences, and She was always ready for more. Every adverse circumstance became nourishment for Her spirit to grow in splendor and strength. She never failed to learn a new lesson from any situation in life. That is why today Her life shines like the North Star, guiding countless lost souls.

Amma not only has this capacity Herself, but She also helps us to develop this capacity. During one of Amma's programs in Her ashram in San Ramon, California, there was an accidental fire in the ashram kitchen and some devotees suffered burn injuries. Amma, the swamis, and many other devotees went to see them in the hospital, giving moral support and praying for them. Amma also spoke to them on the phone many times. Though they suffered physically, their minds were not negatively affected because of Amma's love and concern. In fact, all of them were back in the kitchen when Amma visited San Ramon the next time, and they had even more enthusiasm and dedication than ever.

When I was talking with them, they told me that their faith in Amma had deepened after the fire because they had felt Amma's presence, grace, strength, and support throughout their difficulties. They also knew that if the accident had happened in some other place or at some other time, they would not have recovered so quickly from their shock, pain and suffering. Many of them said that each time Amma would call them or send them some prasad through other devotees, they would gain fresh bouts of energy and strength. They knew that it was their prarabdha karma to suffer like this, and that such an accident would have happened wherever they might have been. Since it happened when Amma was near them, they were able to receive Amma's personal attention and consolation, which greatly helped to ease their suffering.

One of the affected devotees said, "The fire has injured our bodies but not our faith and spirit. In fact, it has increased our faith." Without taking the accident in a negative way or dwelling on their fate, they saw the accident as an opportunity to grow and rededicate their lives at Amma's feet. They did not let it become a stumbling block in their lives, but instead transformed it into a stepping-stone for their spiritual growth.

CATCH-22

As spiritual seekers, we are all interested in spiritual growth. We want to progress in spiritual practices such as meditation or chanting mantras, and we know how important it is to have a calm and quiet mind during these spiritual practices. Many people who start these practices become disappointed because they are not able to silence their minds. It is very important for a seeker to understand what the factors are that affect the mind during meditation.

Most of us engage in a spiritual practice for a period of time each day while the rest of the day we are engaged in a wide variety of activities—managing household affairs, performing our work-related duties, studying, watching TV, going to the movies, etc. Many of these worldly activities are not conducive to meditation. In fact, their impact disturbs our mind and jeopardizes the results gained through meditation.

It is like mixing salt with sugar. The sugar is the sweetness derived from meditation and other spiritual practices. The salt is the impact of external actions. We can't enjoy the sweetness from a mixture of salt and sugar. When our meditation is influenced by our daily activities, we are unable to experience the fruit of our meditation. Amma gives an example of an escalator that is moving in the opposite direction that we want to go. No matter how fast we walk, we will make little progress.

We thus find ourselves in a Catch-22 situation. If we continue performing external actions, many of these activities will hinder us from experiencing the fruits of our meditation. But if we give up those activities, we cannot earn a livelihood, and without a livelihood, how can we meditate peacefully? So what is the solution?

All our actions have an impact on our meditation, directly or indirectly. Some actions offer a positive effect and others a negative one. The solution is to try to convert each action into worship of the Divine. Try to remember God in every action. Having this mindful attitude toward all our daily activities will help us in our meditation.

TURNING WORK INTO WORSHIP

If we look at Amma's early life, we can see how She transformed every household chore into a form of worship. She was engaged in many activities that are generally considered non-spiritual: cooking for the family; cleaning the house; doing the laundry; bringing water from a public tap and tending the cows. Because of Her attitude, Amma was able to convert this routine housework into worship of God. While preparing food for Her family, She had the attitude that She was cooking for Lord Krishna. While cleaning the house, She would imagine She was cleaning the house to welcome Krishna. While washing Her family's clothes, Amma would imagine She was washing Krishna's clothes. Because She had pure love and devotion toward Krishna, She was able to put Her heart and soul into this work, without ever feeling bored or fed up. She always prayed for more and more work, so that She could serve Krishna to Her heart's content. None of the abuse She faced from Her parents or from others could affect Her inner joy in serving Her beloved Krishna to the best of Her abilities.

If we have that love and devotion toward God or the Guru, we can also experience that inner joy. We can improve the quality of our work and meditation, and live our lives filled with love and happiness. Once we train our mind to look at every object as belonging to God or Amma, and we have the attitude that whatever work we do is an opportunity to be of service to Him or Her, then it becomes possible to attain this synergy through our work and meditation.

If we do our work and duties with this attitude of devotion, we can also overcome many of our negative tendencies.

When I worked in a bank, I used to get angry with the customers, especially with people who looked like uneducated villagers. If anyone made a mistake in completing a form to withdraw or deposit money, I would get irritated. This habit continued for a few years even after I came to Amma. After hearing Amma's loving instructions, I felt that I must discard this bad habit of mine. I tried many times, but I always failed.

One day I went to Amma and told Her about my short temper and asked Her how to overcome it. Amma gave me a very simple method. She asked me if there was anyone I loved and respected. I remembered one of my most outstanding professors and also one of my previous bank managers, whom I not only loved and respected but also visited frequently. I told Amma about these two people. Amma then asked me, "If they were to send someone to you to get some work done for them at your bank, what would you do?" I said I would greet them warmly and do anything necessary to help them. Then Amma asked, "And what if Amma sent someone to you?" I replied that if I knew Amma had sent someone to me, I would serve them with love, and I would give them tea and snacks as well! Amma said, "There you are. From tomorrow onwards, when you are at the bank, dealing with customers, imagine that Amma is sending each one of those customers to you. If you really love Me, you will treat them lovingly; you won't get angry with anyone, even if they make mistakes. From tomorrow onward, try this method."

I was very happy to hear such a simple solution, little knowing how difficult it would be to put into practice. I failed many times to practice Amma's advice, and after becoming aware of my mistake I would apologize to the person with whom I'd lost my temper. Every day, before starting my work, I would pray to Amma to give me strength and patience. After a few months I was able to overcome my short-tempered nature to a great extent. Also, I started feeling happy because I was succeeding in practicing Amma's teaching. Within a couple of years, dealing with the customers with love and a smile became easy for me.

Previously, I had felt I was wasting my time in the bank while the other brahmacharis were doing their spiritual practices at the ashram. This feeling of frustration had also been one of the reasons for my being short-tempered toward the customers. After receiving such an effective method of remembering how to treat everyone lovingly, I knew I was doing my spiritual practice at the bank. With each customer who left smiling because of my kindness, I felt happy knowing I was following Amma's instructions and cultivating a worshipful attitude in my work.

RIGHT UNDERSTANDING AND RIGHT ATTITUDE

There was a farmer who had a large farm. He went to the hardware store to buy a saw to cut down some trees in his orchard. The salesman showed him the latest saw and told him that he could cut down fifty trees in one hour. Of course the saw was expensive, but the farmer decided to purchase it. A week later, he returned to the store with a complaint. "This saw is defective," he told the salesman. "You told me I could cut down fifty trees in one hour, but I couldn't even cut down ten in one hour." The salesman took the saw from the farmer and plugged the cord into the socket to test it. He turned it on, and immediately it made a loud buzzing sound. The farmer was surprised. "Wait a second! What's that sound? I never heard that sound when I was using it."

The farmer had been using the electric saw as a manual one! He was using the saw without plugging it into a socket. The farmer simply lacked the proper understanding.

We need a good understanding of why we are doing spiritual practices and how our actions influence these spiritual practices. Through right understanding and the right attitude, most of the actions we do will support our spiritual practices. Amma says that with the right attitude, our actions can be converted into worship.

Once we assume the role of a householder, we have a lot of responsibilities. To discharge our responsibilities toward our family with love and sincerity, without expecting anything in return, is a way of worshipping God or Amma. If we perform these tasks as a way of pleasing Amma or God, it will help us in our spiritual practice.

At times, even though we do our duties sincerely for the family, we may not get a positive response from them. They may not appreciate our efforts and may even misunderstand us and behave rudely toward us. Yet, if we are sincere in our heart, and we perform our duties as an offering to God or Amma, we will be helped tremendously in our spiritual progress.

There are two results for every action. One can be seen while the other cannot be seen. When we help somebody— for example, when we give food to a hungry person—we may see that person's happy and contented face, as his or her hunger is appeased. The unseen effect is the merit or the good karma that accumulates to our credit because of this positive action. And this merit will bear fruit in due course.

Similarly, there are two effects when a murderer kills somebody. The seen effect is that the victim dies. The unseen effect is the sin or the bad karma that the murderer incurs; and this will invariably haunt and afflict the murderer, even if he or she is able to escape from the law.

Whether or not our positive words and actions are appreciated by anyone, the benefit of the invisible effect will always come to us in the future. This is the advantage of discharging our duties and responsibilities sincerely.

We tend to like some of our responsibilities and dislike others. One parent doesn't like helping the children with homework, while the other parent doesn't like carrying out the garbage. We like to play with our children when they are laughing, but we don't want to deal with them when they are crying.

There was a couple that had a son who cried very often. Every time he cried, the boy's mother would come running, but the father would ignore the boy's crying. Finally, the mother exclaimed to the father, "Why don't you go and comfort him sometimes? He is half your son, after all."

The boy's father replied, "Yes, but my half is the quiet half!"

When we have likes and dislikes, our mind becomes agitated. As a consequence, our meditation is disturbed. It is important to remove our likes and dislikes as much as possible. If our responsibilities are discharged with the right attitude and understanding, these duties can help us overcome our likes and dislikes.

There was a young man who had just joined Amma's ashram. He wanted to be a brahmachari. However, he was not interested in chanting a mantra. He felt that it was a boring exercise to keep chanting the same words again and again. Amma always says that we should try to chant our mantra as many times as possible. Knowing about his aversion toward chanting a mantra, Amma gave him the job of answering the telephone calls at the information and reception counter. All the phone calls had to be answered manually as we did not have the luxury of an answering machine.

In the ashram, when we pick up the telephone, we usually say, "Om Namah Shivaya," and not "Hello," or "Hi." And when we hang up, then also we say, "Om Namah Shivaya." We don't say, "Bye." We all know that

"Om Namah Shivaya" is a powerful mantra. It means, "I bow down to the Eternally Auspicious One." So this spiritual aspirant had to say, "Om Namah Shivaya," every time he picked up and hung up the phone. Thus, each day he would have to say, "Om Namah Shivaya," 100 times or even more. And since the phone lines were inadequate in those days, the connection was often poor. So the brahmachari would have to shout, "Om Namah Shivaya!" a few extra times. In this way he would chant the mantra hundreds of times in a day. Though he was saying, "Om Namah Shivaya," so many times a day, he was not aware that he was chanting a mantra. Eventually, by doing his duty well, the brahmachari overcame his dislike toward chanting his mantra. Finally, one day he went and asked Amma to initiate him with the "Om Namah Shivaya" mantra.

Whether we are a businessperson, a worker, a householder, a politician or a doctor, if we perform our duties as an offering to the Divine, we can, to a great extent, overcome our likes and dislikes. This will help us in our meditation, because the fewer likes and dislikes we have, the calmer and quieter the mind will be, and meditation will then be easier for us.

When likes and dislikes are conquered, it is easier to see God in everything. No longer will we judge a person as someone we like or dislike. Normally we like or love a person because of our delusion and attachment, and we dislike a person due to our egoism, jealousy and other such negative qualities that prevent us from seeing the divinity in that person.

Even at the age of ten, Amma was mature enough to comprehend right understanding and right attitude. In the village there were many elderly people who had been discarded by their families. Some of them were sick. Others had terrible contagious skin diseases, and even their own families avoided them. But Amma would go to them. She talked with them lovingly, bathed them, washed their clothes and fed them. When Her parents reprimanded Her for wasting Her time in this way, She would say, "I don't consider serving these people as a waste of time because I don't see them as different from God. Through serving them, I am serving God."

Amma often says, "The sun does not need the help of a candlelight. Likewise God does not need anything from us. God is not sitting somewhere up above the clouds; God dwells in all creatures. So, by serving others, especially the poor and suffering, we are actually serving God."

APPRECIATING GOD IN EVERYTHING

One day, a mischievous boy from the neighborhood was caught stealing some gold jewelry and cash from the ashram office. At that time the financial condition of the ashram was very challenging, and this boy had been warned many times by the ashram residents. So when he was caught stealing again, some of us were very angry. We tied his hands behind his back and took him to Amma thinking that She would give him a good scolding. Seeing the boy, Amma broke into a smile and suddenly it seemed as though Amma was in a different world.

We waited more than fifteen minutes, but there was no response from Amma. So, we let the boy go, giving him a severe warning. Later, Amma told us that when the boy stood in front of Her with his hands tied behind him, She was reminded of Baby Krishna. When Lord Krishna was a child, he used to steal butter and milk from the homes of the milkmaids. The neighbors complained to Krishna's foster mother, Yashoda. Every day she would hear new stories about Krishna's antics. The complaints increased day by day, until, finally, it became too much for her. She tied Krishna's hands behind his back and scolded him with a show of anger.

Many western readers may be interested to know why Lord Krishna acted as a "butter thief." In Brindavan, where Krishna lived as a child, the gopis were poor milkmaids, who earned their livelihood by selling milk and butter. Krishna saw that all their thoughts revolved around these milk products. So, even though he got as much as he wanted in his own house, he went out to the houses of the gopis and stole their milk, curd and butter. The gopis loved him so much that every day each gopi wished that Krishna would steal from her house on that day. The gopis also enjoyed telling each other and Krishna's mother about his frolics. In this way, Krishna soon became the central figure of all the thoughts and conversations of the gopis. Thus, effortlessly, the gopis could meditate on Krishna throughout the day. So, by stealing their butter, Krishna really stole the gopis' hearts.

When Amma saw the boy who had stolen from the ashram, She felt that it was Baby Krishna standing in front of Her. So, how could She scold him? Amma was able to see God even in a thief. And the boy was transformed by Her behavior. He never stole again. When Amma saw the godliness in him, She must also have invoked the good qualities hidden within him.

This doesn't mean that we should let criminals do as they please, saying that we see God in them. If someone steals from us or commits some other crime, of course we should protect ourselves and call the police. We should act with discrimination. Even if we see God in a criminal, we may not be able to awaken the godliness in them!

A few days later, I made a mistake and I knew that Amma was going to scold me for it. Having witnessed how Amma saw Krishna in the little thief, I asked a brahmachari to tie my hands behind my back and take me to Amma. I was sure that Amma would see Krishna in me as well. But She just chased me away. Since I was a spiritual seeker, She expected me to have a bit more discrimination and maturity.

During Her early days, anything in nature was sufficient to make Amma go into samadhi. When She would see fish jumping in the backwaters, when She watched the ripples on the surface of the water, when the breeze caressed Her body, She would lose Herself in deep meditation.

I remember an incident that took place at Amma's ashram in San Ramon, California. It was a full moon night. Amma finished Her evening darshan at about two in the morning. We were driving back from the temple to the house where She was to spend the night. She looked up at the full moon and said, "How wonderful it is!" The car continued to the house, and Amma went to Her room. Everyone quietly went to bed. Amma waited for everyone to go to sleep and then slipped out and went up a nearby hill. Later, the brahmacharini who accompanied Amma told us that Amma spent almost four hours dancing in ecstasy in the light of the full moon.

Just the sight of the full moon was enough to send Her into a state of ecstasy. Most of us are not like that. We have all seen so many full moons, even blue moons, but they don't have such an impact on us. Actually, when I see a full moon, it reminds me of a chapatti or pappadam! Why are our reactions so different from Amma's? What is needed for us to become more like Her?

It's all a question of training the mind to make a shift in our attitude and in how we approach our day-to-day activities.

Once there was a group of novice monks being trained in a monastery. After a regular session, they would be given a break. During this break, they could relax, enjoy nature, and spend some time in prayer. It was called the "prayer break." One of the novices hadn't yet given up the habit of smoking. So he asked the priest's permission to smoke during the prayer break. The priest angrily told him that he would be sinning if he smoked during prayer time.

The next day during the prayer break, this novice happened upon another young monk smoking happily, sitting on a rock among the rose bushes in the garden. The first novice, who had been rebuked by the priest, was shocked to see his brother smoking. He asked, "How did you manage to get permission to smoke? When I asked the priest if I could smoke, he was very angry with me."

The smoking novice said, "What, exactly, did you ask the priest?"

He replied, "I asked whether I could smoke during prayer time."

"That was where you made the mistake," the smoking novice said. "I asked whether I could pray while smoking, and the priest said, 'By all means! In fact you should always be praying.'"

Just by shifting his words around, the novice got permission to do what he wanted. Smoking while praying is considered a sin but praying while smoking isn't.

Likewise, a slight shift in our attitude will greatly improve the quality of our spiritual practice. Worldly thoughts during meditation are a hindrance to meditation, whereas thinking about God while doing daily chores is actually helpful to meditation.

So let us try to remember Amma wherever we are and whatever we are doing, so that our whole life becomes meditation. This is the hour. This is the moment. It is not yet too late to start our spiritual journey and progress.

I am reminded of a famous poem:

> *When the daylight shone,*
> *And the market was open*
> *I purchased no wares.*
> *Alas, for me, the night has come,*
> *The shops are closed.*
> *I remember the things I need.*

So wake up.

Let us make use of Amma's grace, Her love and Her compassion.

Her arms are always open, ready to embrace us.

CHAPTER 10

THE PATH OF KNOWLEDGE

THE NATURE OF THE MIND

A seeker following the path of knowledge contemplates on Brahman.[7] He or she meditates on the aphorisms, "I am Brahman; I am the imperishable, eternal Atman. The Self in me is the Self in all beings." According to Lord Krishna, to tread the path of knowledge requires great control over the senses and a tranquil mind. Moreover, the obstacles that a seeker on the path of knowledge faces are great. A seeker who constantly contemplates, "I am Brahman, the Supreme Self," has many chances of becoming egoistic unless he or she has already attained a considerable degree of mental purity, either in this or in previous lives, and has the attitude of total surrender to a living Master. Generally, for those who are deeply steeped in the notion that "I am the body," non-dualistic contemplation becomes a kind of self-deception. These people will say, "Why should I obey or bow down to anyone? I am Brahman." They forget that others are also Brahman. They fail to realize the spirit of this great saying.

---

[7] *Brahman* is the formless, attributeless, impersonal Truth. Brahman is considered to be the absolute Reality.

Thus, the pitfalls are many, and the seeker of the formless aspect of God has to be extremely careful.

In the *Bhagavad Gita* (Chapter VI, Verse 34), Arjuna and Lord Krishna have a discussion about the nature of the mind.

Arjuna says:

> cañcalaṁ hi manaḥ Kṛṣṇa
> pramāthi balavad dṛḍham
> tasyā 'haṁ nigrahaṁ manye
> vāyor iva suduṣkaram

> *O Krishna, you are saying so many things about equa-nimity of mind and disciplining the mind, but I find my mind totally restless, terrible and unyielding. Struggling to control this mind is like trying to rein in the winds. What can I do?*

Krishna replies,

> asaṁśayaṁ mahābāho
> mano durnigrahaṁ calam
> abhyāsena tu kaunteya
> vairāgyeṇa ca gṛhyate

> *Yes, what you say is true. The mind is restless, terrible and unyielding. Restraining the mind is as difficult as restraining the wind, but through practice and by cultivating dispassion, it is possible to bring it under control.*

The mind is often compared to a monkey, and sometimes to a drunk monkey, because the mind is so naughty and restless. Baby monkeys are especially naughty. Imagine that the most mischievous monkey gets stung by a scorpion. You can imagine how restless it will be! Our minds are even worse than that. We can see this when we meditate. The best time to watch the mind is when we meditate. At other times we are not aware of what our mind is doing. As an experiment, try to sit for ten minutes in solitude with a notebook and write down all your thoughts during those ten minutes. You will be surprised at what you find. Our ideas are often unconnected and unrelated to each other, jumping from one subject to another or from one person to the next without any rhyme or reason.

We feel so blissful during sleep, when the mind is not at work. It is possible to attain that stillness of mind even while we are awake, if we can learn to control the mind and think only what we want to think. The mind has the capacity to focus at our direction. We have to train it. Training the mind is very difficult, but it is possible through constant practice.

PRACTICE AND DISPASSION

The restlessness of the mind comes mainly from its likes and dislikes, or preferences. These preferences are expressed as attachment or repulsion toward objects, persons or situations. Repulsion is simply the negative form of attachment. Today our mind is like a feather tossed about by the currents of winds from all directions. To still the mind, we have to free it from the push and pull of likes and dislikes.

Even if there is external turbulence around us, we can enjoy a great deal of peace if our mind is free from internal disturbances. Our internal disturbances are mainly due to the negativities in our mind. We have to become conscious of the burden of carrying these negative tendencies or feelings. Only then will we want to get rid of them. At some point in time, we have to overcome our defects, and since the internal disturbances are the most powerful disruptions to inner peace, we need to conquer these defects sooner rather than later.

To gain freedom from internal disturbances, we have to discipline our mind. The practice required to restrain and control the mind is challenging at first, for we usually want to give the mind a free rein. However, in time, we will actually begin to like the process of disciplining the mind.

I remember a famous story. In India it is a custom for householders to invite sannyasis into their homes to feed them. They consider it a source of merit to do so. According to Indian tradition, a full course meal consists of dishes with six different tastes—sweet, sour, pungent, salty, spicy and bitter. In some homes, they also serve bitter gourd along with other dishes. Sannyasis are supposed to accept both sweet and bitter things with equanimity.

A sannyasi was once invited to a house where they had prepared a full course meal. It was a sumptuous meal that included bitter gourd. There was only one thing in life that this sannyasi hated, and that was bitter gourd. He couldn't stand it, but now that he had accepted the invitation and had gone to the house, he had to respect the custom. He couldn't say, "I don't like bitter gourd." He was supposed to like all types of food equally. So he thought, "There are other delicious dishes here, so let me eat the bitter gourd first. Once I am done with it, I can relax and enjoy the other dishes. I don't want to eat the bitter gourd with the other foods and spoil their taste." So he finished the bitter gourd first.

The lady of the house was watching as the sannyasi ate, and as soon as he finished the bitter gourd, she served him another big scoop of that vegetable. The sannyasi thought, "Oh no! I think today's my bad day." With great difficulty, he finished eating the second serving. He cursed himself for having visited that house. Had he known that they had prepared bitter gourd, he would have told them he was fasting that day, but it was too late. The sannyasi's suffering didn't end there. The woman, who by now was convinced that this sannyasi liked bitter gourd very much, put one more scoop of bitter gourd on his plate. You can imagine the condition of the sannyasi! Cursing his star, the sannyasi somehow finished his meal, vowing mentally never to return to that house again.

The lady host immediately called the next house where the sannyasi was supposed to go for his night bhiksha (alms), telling them that the sannyasi loved bitter gourd. She suggested that they cook some special curries with bitter gourd when he came to their home for bhiksha. From then on, the news spread and everybody prepared bitter gourd whenever they invited this sannyasi. Finally, he got so used to it that he began to like the vegetable, even though he'd had such an aversion to it initially.

Similarly, if we keep eating the bitter gourd of practicing restraint of the mind, we will grow to like the practice.

SPIRITUAL STRENGTH

There are generally three aspects of our being that determine how we deal with the world, with other people, and with the different experiences of life. They are our physical, emotional (mental), and intellectual aspects. There is another one as well: our spiritual aspect. For most of us, the spiritual aspect remains in a dormant state, because most of the time we focus on the first three aspects of our being.

If we focus only on these three aspects, we will be subject to a roller coaster of emotions and desires. We crave so many things in the world and we have numerous needs. Some of those needs and desires are beyond our means and our capacity, and are never fulfilled. As a result of this shortfall, we become disappointed, frustrated and dejected. Our frustration may increase until we finally lose all our mental strength. A person who is mentally weak won't be able to face even small challenges in life. Just a minor incident will be enough to upset him or her. Amma says, "Even a tiny ant can upset such a person."

Once, a friend of mine bought a new house. A few days after he moved in, he saw some ants in the kitchen. This upset him a bit because it was a brand new house. He wondered where the ants were coming from. To make matters worse, within a short time hundreds of ants were crawling in his kitchen. He was getting more upset now, scratching his head and wondering what to do about this problem. So he ran to a nearby shop to buy a container of insecticide. Unfortunately, only one container of insecticide was available, and it was slightly damaged. He asked if he could get a discount because the container was damaged, but the shopkeeper refused. The man got into an argument with the shopkeeper, demanding a discount.

He was already upset about the ants in his kitchen, and now he was getting more upset because of the argument with the shopkeeper. They continued to argue until finally they almost came to blows. They ended up going to court to settle the dispute. All this happened just because of a few ants!

Amma says that until a few centuries ago, people had very strong minds. They were not troubled mentally. As the years went by, people stopped adhering to their dharma, and their values slowly deteriorated. As a result, people became greedier and more selfish. They became mentally weak due to lack of discipline and discrimination. They no longer knew how to face various situations in life. Their minds became tense and agitated; they underwent a lot of stress. Nowadays, countless people are mentally weak and even neurotic.

The only remedy other than psychiatric treatment is to become spiritually awakened. This awakening will balance the physical, emotional and intellectual aspects within us, so that we can live in harmony. In the presence of a great soul like Amma, it is easy for us to awaken our spiritual potential. Once this takes place, our minds will become strong and subtle, and we will be able to look at our lives with far more clarity.

I would like to narrate an incident from Amma's life, which shows the kind of spiritual strength She had even as a young girl.

Because Amma spent so much time washing clothes, cleaning, washing the cows, carrying water, etc., Her clothes were wet most of the time. One day Amma's dress was completely drenched, so She borrowed Her sister's dress. When Amma's mother, Damayanti, saw this, she got angry and scolded Amma. She said, "You don't deserve to wear such good clothes! How dare you wear that dress?" Saying this, Damayanti snatched the dress from Amma's hands and walked away, making Amma wear Her old clothes.

We can only imagine what would have been our state of mind if we were placed in that situation. But Amma didn't feel sad. She thought, "Perhaps God doesn't want me to wear that dress, so, from now on, I'm not going to wear any new or good clothes unless God brings me something. Until then, I'll wear only old clothes that have been discarded by others."

From that day on, Amma wore only clothes that Her family members no longer wanted. One day Amma was wearing an old, discarded blouse that happened to have a colorful design. Amma's older brother didn't like this. He scolded Her, accusing Her of wearing a colorful blouse just to attract the attention of young men. He ordered Her to take it off and then he set it on fire right in front of Her. Amma was not angry or upset because She thought it must be God's will. From that day on, Amma wore only white clothes.

In contrast to the lives of Buddha, Krishna and Rama, who all had a royal or aristocratic upbringing, the conditions of Amma's early life were miserable. But because of Her attitude of surrender to God, Amma didn't succumb to Her circumstances. Nor has She been affected by Her present status as an internationally acclaimed spiritual leader. Amma has always been a perfect example of simplicity and humility. And She is easily available and accessible. Even now that Amma has been recognized worldwide, She does not live a luxurious life by any means. She takes the minimum for Herself and gives the maximum to people who need Her help, guidance, blessings and grace.

THREE WAYS OF SPIRITUAL AWAKENING

Amma is fully established in divine consciousness. Because the spiritual potential within Her is fully awakened, our own spiritual awakening occurs more easily in

Her presence. Amma's touch, glance, or thought can awaken us spiritually. By Her mere will, Amma can awaken our spiritual potential. The scriptures refer to just such a phenomenon—a true Master can spiritually awaken anyone by touch, glance or thought.

Interestingly, legend has it that this is how a hen, a fish, and a tortoise hatch their eggs. A hen hatches her eggs by sitting on them; the eggs hatch due to the heat produced by the constant touch of the mother hen's body. In a similar way, Amma can awaken the spiritual potential in us just by touching us. Living constantly in the company of a Master, the heat of discipline slowly develops and purifies the mind, causing the shell of the ego to break so that the Self can emerge.

According to traditional Indian belief, a fish spawns its eggs and then stares intently at the eggs. Due to the intensity of the fish's gaze, the eggs hatch. Every single glance from Amma helps to awaken the spiritual potential within us. Just as the lotus bud blossoms when the rays of the sun fall on it, our closed hearts open up when Amma's glance falls on us.

The tortoise lays its eggs on the shore and then returns to the water and thinks about the eggs. According to legend, the eggs will hatch due to the intensity of the tortoise's thoughts. In the same way, Amma can awaken our spiritual potential with Her sankalpa. Just as a remote control device can control many machines, Amma's thought waves can control the events of our lives if we tune our hearts with Hers.

Without our even being aware of it, Amma resolves many of our prarabdha karmas and innate tendencies. Just as a kite takes off when there is a good breeze and expert hands controlling the strings, we can soar up into the skies of spirituality when our spiritual practices are augmented by the blessings and grace of a great Master like Amma.

THE BENEFITS OF ATTAINING THE STATE OF YOGA

The ability to recognize the harmful effects of an action or a habit can motivate us to overcome that negative habit. Likewise, the ability to recognize the beneficial effects of an action will motivate us to cultivate the habit of positive actions. The highest goal is attaining the state of Yoga. The state of Yoga is the ultimate union with God or the Truth. There are many benefits of attaining this state.

Stillness of the mind

The mind of a person who has attained the state of Yoga is tranquil, one-pointed and free of vacillations. This tranquility is not the result of the fulfillment of desires. If it were, the tranquility would be fleeting, because when one desire is fulfilled, another arises. If that desire in turn cannot be fulfilled, then the tranquility will be lost. Real tranquility is the result of a steady practice of meditation. One who has attained this state of Yoga is capable of maintaining stillness of mind, despite his or her activities and responsibilities. Look at Amma. She is the head of a large number of institutions and gives personal counseling to millions without ever taking a holiday. When necessary, She puts on a show of different emotions, but in the depth of Her mind there is always calmness. This can be compared to the waves on the surface of the ocean; deep inside there is only stillness. Stillness of mind is one characteristic of the state of Yoga.

Seeing the Self in oneself

Those who are established in Yoga see the Self in themselves. They do not ever lose sight of the Self. Such a person sees the Self in other beings as well. In our present state of awareness, we think that we are separate from the world and the people around us. We love some people, dislike some people, and have no particular feelings toward the others. A *Yogi* (one who has attained the ultimate state of Yoga) is one who does not consider anyone as different from him- or herself in essence, who has no attachment or aversion to anyone or anything in particular, and who loves one and all equally. One may be a bad person, an angry person, an impatient person, or a wicked person. All these differences are at the level of the mind. The soul is ever pure and is in no way different from that of a sage or saint. Consciousness is not tainted by any of our qualities or actions.

If I say that my mind is clear or confused, that means there is something apart from my mind that witnesses the condition of my mind. And what is this witness? It is the Atman or Self, which is beyond the mind. This awareness is conscious of everything, but is not affected by anything. Just because my mind is confused, it doesn't mean that my consciousness has become confused. It is just like a screen. You may show a good or a vulgar movie on the screen. Is the screen affected? Not at all. But without a screen the movie cannot be seen. So without consciousness the mind cannot function. The nature of the mind doesn't affect the consciousness, just as the movie doesn't affect the screen.

This pure consciousness without limitations is called the Self or Atman. Once we are established in the Self, which is all-pervading, all-knowing, and all-powerful, we will see only the Self everywhere and in everyone. Then we won't need anything in order to be contented, because we will be content in our own Self.

The experience of bliss

A person established in Yoga experiences infinite bliss. We are all familiar with happiness and unhappiness. Happiness is a state of mind depending on objects, circumstances or other people. When there is happiness, there is also invariably the possibility of unhappiness. If we are happy when we get something, we will be unhappy if we lose that same thing. If our happiness depends on the love of a person, we are sure to be unhappy when that person no longer loves us. Bliss is beyond the pair of opposites. Bliss has no opposite. Bliss is the nature of the Self. It doesn't depend on any outside objects or situations.

Happiness and unhappiness belong to the mind, but bliss is beyond the mind; it comes from the knowledge that "I am of the nature of bliss."

Sometimes Amma would laugh continuously for hours. Sometimes She would cry. I once saw Amma crying like this and I asked Her, "Amma, why are you crying? Is there something that is troubling you? Why are you sad?"

Amma replied, "Who said I was sad?" It was only bliss She felt—a bliss expressed through Her tears. A person established in the Self will enjoy bliss at all times, wherever he or she may be.

> yogarato vā bhogarato vā
> sangarato vā sangavihīnah
> yasya brahmani ramate cittam
> nandati nandati nandatyeva

> *Whether immersed in yoga (spiritual union) or bhoga (outward enjoyment), in companionship or solitude, one whose mind revels in Brahman enjoys bliss.*

> — *Bhaja Govindam,* Verse 19

Abiding in absolute reality

A person established in Yoga abides in absolute reality. According to the philosophy of Vedanta, there are three levels of reality. They are known as apparent reality (*pratibhasika satta*), relative reality (*vyavaharika satta*) and absolute reality (*paramartika satta*).

I see a rope in semi-darkness and mistake it for a snake. That is the apparent reality for me. Another person may see the same rope and think it is a garland. That is the apparent reality for that person. Such personal viewpoints, which relate to the appearance of objects but which actually have nothing to do with the objects themselves, are all classified as apparent reality. Dreams also fall under this category.

Seeing a rope as a rope is known as relative reality. All those whose vision is not distorted will agree it is a rope and not a snake. They won't fear the rope and run away from it; nor will they try to garland someone with it. They will use the rope to tie something. The world as we correctly perceive it, as science and technology describe it, is known as relative reality. It is called relative reality because in its present form it won't last forever—it is subject to change. All relative objects are subject to the six forms of changes: birth, growth, existence, transformation, decay and death. All our worldly relationships, positions, and possessions are in the realm of relative reality.

The third reality is the absolute Truth, which does not undergo any change in the past, present or future. The Self or Atman pervading the whole Creation is the only absolute reality. Being established in absolute reality means realizing that "I am one with the Self."

Infinite gain

There is nothing that is comparable to Self-realization. In this regard, the scriptures say, "Having attained the Self, there is nothing else to be attained." That is why it's called "infinite gain." Self-realized Masters don't want anything; they have gained whatever there is to be gained. For such a person, there is no gain that can be considered superior.

Being unaffected by even the greatest of sorrows

Once we attain this state of Yoga, we won't be affected by any type of sorrow. All sorrows and suffering belong to the world of duality. In other words, sorrows and suffering belong to the body and mind. A person established in the

Self clearly knows that he or she is the pure Self, and not the body, mind or intellect. Such a person goes beyond all opposite pairs, such as pain and pleasure, sorrow and happiness, and likes and dislikes.

In the *Bhagavad Gita*, Lord Krishna gives a unique definition of Yoga. He says, "Dissociation from association with sorrow is Yoga." The word Yoga is derived from the root "*yuj*." It has two meanings. One is "connecting or uniting two things." Thus, when two things unite, it is Yoga. The second meaning is "control, stopping, mastering." In the first sense, Yoga is the union of the mind and the Self. In the second sense, it is controlling or stopping the mind from associating with pain and sorrow.

It is the nature of an untrained mind to always associate with pain and sorrow. We rarely think about how happy or successful we are. Even billionaires have their own share of worries and sorrows. When their minds are fixed on those negative things, they forget that they are billionaires. There are so many good things in life. We have to consciously and deliberately train our minds to always hold on to the positive side of life. One who is established in Yoga does not identify with pain or sorrow.

One who is established in Yoga can also transcend physical pain. We can see Amma continuously giving darshan to any number of people regardless of Her aching body or some other health problem. Even when the 100th person kneels right on Her foot, puts his or her whole body weight on Her lap or hits Her cheek with his or her head while bowing down to narrate some personal woes,

Amma's sweet smile and compassionate words never cease. Amma consciously disassociates Her mind from the pain and aches of the body.

Just as we give importance to our food, sleep, family and other things in life, we should give at least equal importance, if not more, to our spiritual practices. Amma always says meditation is like gold. Even if you can only meditate for ten minutes, that is valuable. Even a single moment spent in meditation is not a waste. Those who are already doing spiritual practices can increase the duration or do them with more intensity, more determination. That is the only way we can gain strength of mind and proceed toward our goal. We are engaged in so many things in life that pull our mind down. To elevate the mind, we must have some sort of spiritual practices such as japa, meditation, listening to or singing bhajans, attending *satsangs* (spiritual talks or discussions) or reading spiritual books. All these practices can give us inspiration and help us to maintain continuous remembrance of God. With a Satguru like Amma, it is possible for any of us to reach the state of Yoga. May Amma bless all of us to reach that supreme state.

CHAPTER 11

PERFORMANCE OF DUTY

DUTY MAINTAINS HARMONY

Modern physics says that the universe moves toward chaos by the law of entropy, whereas Hindu scriptures say that there is a pre-established harmony in the universe and that evolution is a progression toward universal order and harmony. All living beings have a role to play in maintaining this harmony. This harmony is called by different names such as *logos*, dharma or the Tao. Animals and plants do not disturb this harmony, because they live according to their instincts (innate nature). On the other hand, human beings, with their freedom of choice, can either contribute to or disturb this harmony.

A Satguru like Amma works to restore the lost dharma and harmony in the universe. Whatever the Satguru does will only contribute to the harmony in Creation. Thus, whatever they do is right, though it may seem to be otherwise to us.

Amma says every one of us has a duty depending on our role in society. If we do not do our duty properly, chaos and confusion result. If a doctor does not perform his or her duty, the patients will suffer. If a police officer is not doing his or her duty properly, the crime rate will increase.

Similarly, if the members of a family refuse to play their role well, there will be disharmony in the family.

Amma gives the following examples: We may be a householder with a husband or wife and children. When we fulfill our duties toward our family members by loving and taking care of them, discharging all our responsibilities to each one sincerely, we are in tune with the symphony of Creation. Then there will be harmony in the family. A family is a small unit in this Creation. Likewise, there are millions of families in the universe. When all the family members perform their duties appropriately, then there is harmony. It is the same with politicians, businesspeople, workers, military officers, or monks—every person has a unique part to play in this orchestra. When everyone performs his or her duty, there is no disturbance in the harmony of Creation.

In order to maintain dharma, everyone in society should have this attitude. If a politician is sincerely helping and serving the people, then he or she is contributing to the harmony. Similarly, if a businessperson does his or her business without cheating people and takes only reasonable profits, or if a doctor treats patients with love and sympathy, they are in fact worshipping God even though they may not be doing anything that can be labeled as spiritual or religious. But when a politician exploits the people, or when a doctor charges exorbitant fees, this creates disharmony—it goes against dharma.

Amma says that when you play your role in accordance with your duty or dharma, you are naturally contributing to the harmony of the universe. Each individual is like a spoke or a cog in the wheel of Creation. If just one spoke or cog is broken or damaged, it will affect the movement of the wheel. Of course we may not feel it or be aware of it, because the universe is so vast. However, in a small unit we can experience the disharmony. For example, if we put a spoonful of salt in a small cup of water we can taste the saltiness. If we put the same amount of salt in a big bucket of water, we won't taste the salt. This doesn't mean that there is no salt in the water—we are simply not able to perceive it.

Thus, by doing my duty, I am contributing to the harmony and well-being of the world. By not doing my duty, I am causing disharmony, which is the cause of pain and suffering in this world. So when I disturb the harmony, it is like going against God. And when I am contributing to the harmony, it is a way of worshipping God.

Whether we like it or not, we have to discharge our duties and responsibilities without attachment or aversion. This is the difficult part, and we very often need the help of a Guru to succeed at this.

I would like to relate an incident about a western devotee who came to the ashram. This quiet, gentle man had a deep love for Amma. In those days, when there was some seva project in the ashram in which Amma was going to participate, a bell would ring indicating that Amma was "out and about" and everyone could join Her. There was no particular schedule for this kind of seva. Whenever there was a need or an emergency, Amma would come out to take the lead in finishing the task, and others would happily join Her, be it day or night, sun or rain. Many residents loved helping Amma with seva at night because when the work was done, Amma used to prepare coffee and roasted peanuts and distribute these to the residents. Afterwards, She would gather everyone around Her and tell stories and jokes and give satsang.

During this westerner's first night at the ashram, the seva bell sounded at 1:00 in the morning. He didn't come for seva and was annoyed that his sleep was disturbed at that odd hour by the sound of the bell and all the hustle and bustle. The next morning, he was sitting with a long face during Amma's darshan. He complained to Amma about how difficult it was to get a good night's sleep if the bells rang and people were expected to get up in the middle of the night. From that day on, he started sleeping with earplugs.

After seeing everyone doing seva for a few days, he also wanted to help out in some way. So he opted for a regular seva. The assignment he got was working in the kitchen, the noisiest area of the ashram. This man, who preferred everything to be quiet both day and night, was taken aback at the idea of working in such a noisy place, but he was determined to please Amma with his service. So he reported for duty. The first few days, he found it very difficult to bear the noise and the crowd. After a while, his preference for external silence diminished, and eventually, he didn't mind the noise at all. Finally, a day came when he would jokingly say that if there wasn't any noise at night, he couldn't sleep! His love for Amma and adherence to duty helped him overcome his likes and dislikes. For the first time he tasted inner silence, which is unaffected by external noises or clamor. Previously, he couldn't sleep if he heard any noise. Now he can sleep in the midst of loud noise as peacefully as in a quiet Himalayan cave.

So the performance of duty is very important. That is why the Guru assigns specific duties to us. When a doctor, who is used to working in a sterile atmosphere with utmost hygiene, joins the ashram, he or she may be asked to work in the cowshed. At first the doctor may dislike it, but over a period of time this aversion will slowly die away and the individual may start loving the job. Then Amma may put the doctor back to work in the hospital. At this stage, he or she will be able to look at poor patients, dirty and in rags, with an empathetic heart. Such training cannot be received in any medical college.

One of the brahmacharis was asked to take care of the cows when he joined the ashram. He was an academically well-qualified person. So he protested to Amma, saying that he had come to the ashram to do spiritual practices and to learn scriptures. He also said he had not come to the ashram to waste his life by taking care of the cows.

After a month or so, a great scholar came to the ashram. Some of us requested that he offer classes on the *Srimad Bhagavatam*. One day as he was narrating a passage, he talked about serving cows, the favorite animals of Lord Krishna. The passage said that taking care of a cow is a sacred seva equal to serving the Lord Himself. In the

Hindu tradition, the cow is considered to be a sacred animal. Whoever refuses the opportunity to serve cows is throwing away a wonderful opportunity to gain the grace of the Lord. The brahmachari who had refused to do the cow seva listened to the passage, realized his mistake, and told Amma that he would lovingly do the cow seva.

However, by then Amma had other plans for this brahmachari. She asked him to do seva in the kitchen. The brahmachari did not like that seva either, but eventually, he felt remorseful and started cleaning the toilets and bathrooms to make amends for his earlier recalcitrant behavior.

No matter what we may feel about the duty we are given, we should perform it without fail. We shouldn't try to find some excuse not to perform our responsibility. The question of whether we like it or not depends on our preferences, but if we do it as our duty, slowly we can overcome our likes and dislikes. That is why Amma sometimes gives us work that we don't like to do. Somehow, either today or tomorrow, we have to overcome our likes and dislikes. If we cling to them, there will always be disturbances in our mind. Such disturbances are detrimental for spiritual seekers because the inner turmoil interferes with our meditation and concentration on spiritual practices. For an ordinary person, the disturbances in the mind may not be a problem, as this person isn't doing any spiritual practice. Such a person may not even be aware of the disturbances in the mind, unless psychological problems develop.

The world will never be according to our liking. We need to learn to like the world the way it is. Only then will we experience peace of mind. Otherwise, however rich and powerful we may be, we'll still have reasons to be sad, tense and agitated. Whatever Amma asks us to do is only to help us overcome our negativity so that we can experience and enjoy inner peace.

THE POWER OF HABITS

Many of us feel inspired to cultivate good habits in Amma's presence because of the example She sets. Even small children feel inspired. The sad fact is that most of us are unable to sustain this inspiration. As soon as we move away from Amma's physical presence, we tend to go back to our old way of life because we find it difficult to cultivate good habits and easy to pick up bad ones. Conversely, it is very easy to give up good habits, and very difficult to give up bad ones. So we deliberately have to practice changing our habits until the practice becomes spontaneous and natural and the good qualities become a habit. Once we acquire a good habit and make it part of our character by willful practice, it becomes very difficult for us to give it up.

The importance of cultivating good habits can be understood from the way they affect our mind. All our spiritual practices are done for the purpose of calming our mind so that Self-knowledge can be attained. Just as the moon is reflected in the calm waters of a lake, the Self is revealed when the mind is calm and quiet. That is why purity of mind is given so much importance. Once we cultivate good habits, we will feel suffocated if we are not able to practice them.

Amma says that the cultivation of good, positive habits is very important because negative habits such as impatience, jealousy, judging and finding fault with others will prevent us from experiencing peace of mind.

The mind picks up habits, especially ones that are negative and unnecessary, and becomes set in its ways. It is not possible to change all those habits in a year or two. The power of our habits is so strong that a great deal of effort is needed to put the mind on the right track.

Amma tells a story that illustrates how powerful our habits are. There was a poor man who went to a sannyasi and said, "I'm a very poor man. Please help me to become rich." The sannyasi blessed him and told him about a beach where precious gemstones could be found. "You can sell them and make a lot of money," said the sannyasi. "The problem is that it's difficult to tell the difference between a gemstone and an ordinary stone. They all look alike and are scattered all over the beach. So you have to be careful. If you hold one of those gemstones in your hand, you will feel the warmth of the stone. Only if you feel the warmth can you be sure it is a precious stone." The poor man immediately went to that beach and set to work. He picked up stone after stone and tested them. Then it occurred to him that if he put each one back on the ground after he had rejected them, they would get mixed up with the other stones and he wouldn't be able to know which ones he had already tested. So, after picking up each stone, he would throw it into the ocean if it wasn't warm.

Day after day, he searched along the beach. Many days passed until finally one day he picked up a stone and felt that it was warm. He was elated to find a precious stone at last. Nevertheless, having felt that the stone was warm, he threw it into the ocean out of habit!

This story shows how overpowered we are by our habits.

This is why Amma says that we should cultivate positive habits. By doing so, we can reduce the strength of our negative habits. Once a habit loses its strength, it is easy to conquer and remove it. In the beginning we may not like the new positive habit and it may take extra effort, but we mustn't give up the effort. And once we start practicing it, whether we actually like it or not doesn't matter; the practice itself will give us strength. This is why Amma says, "Try to chant your mantra, read spiritual books, meditate, listen to bhajans, and take part in satsang." Spiritual practice doesn't mean only meditation; we have choices. Such activities help us to cultivate good qualities and to continuously focus on God.

I may be doing something that is of no use to me, but still I go on doing it because it has become a habit. Before people knew that smoking causes cancer, smoking cigarettes used to be a much more common habit. Now the Surgeon General's warning is on all cigarette packets, saying, "Smoking is injurious to health." Because of this, many people have given up smoking. Even people who used to smoke many packs a day have been able to stop because they are now aware of the dangers of smoking.

In the same way, when we become aware of the harm or futility in something that we are doing, then we will find the strength to give it up and to change our behavior.

SEVEN VOWS FOR A WEEK

Taking a vow is a great challenge in life—a challenge to our inertia, laziness and procrastination. A vow is like a bridle for the untamed, wild horse of our mind. If we can keep the horse under control, riding is not only enjoyable by itself, but it also takes us to our destination much more quickly than walking. On the other hand, if we mount an unbridled wild horse, the ride will be dreadful and will surely result in disaster or even death.

I remember a famous saying: "Sow a thought, reap an action; sow an action, reap a habit; sow a habit, reap a character." Any routine that is repeated over a period of time becomes a habit. Habits form our character. A person's character is the foundation stone for his or her success in life. However, we all know that it is impossible for us to develop all the good qualities overnight. The only practical option is to cultivate a few good qualities at a time over a longer period, so that they will become our second nature. As a daily bath keeps the body clean and healthy, vows help us to keep our mind clean from the dirt of jealousy, hatred, anger, impatience, etc.

Offered as the ABCs of spiritual life, here are seven vows which are based on Amma's teachings and which can be practiced one at a time, one for each day of the week. The order in which we practice them does not matter; just choose one day in the week for each vow. As pure milk poured into a contaminated vessel turns sour, God's grace, when it descends into an impure mind, cannot be of benefit. These vows help us to purify our mind and also bring it under our control. One specialty of these vows is that the gains of observing them can be experienced without waiting a long time. Take a firm resolve to live by one vow a day. If, by chance, a vow cannot be fulfilled on a particular day, try to carry it out on the same day the following week. Amma says, "The practice of good qualities is also a part of worship. Spirituality without practice is like trying to reside in the blueprint of a house."

Vow for the first day:
Diminish anger. Everyone knows that anger is harmful. Yet, how many among us can live by the vow, "I will never get angry again for as long as I live"? That would be very difficult. To start with, if we make a firm decision to control our anger and our tendency to blame or speak ill of others just for one day a week, it is possible to do so. At least for that day, we will be creating a wonderful atmosphere in our home and at our place of work.

Vow for the second day:

Add a smile. It doesn't take a long time to get beautiful responses from others if we decide to say whatever we have to say with a smile—again, just for one day a week to start with. Even when the situation demands that we shout, scold or nag, we do it with a smile for that day—and right away we will see what a different world that creates. It takes the coordination of more facial muscles to frown than to smile. To smile we need the help of only a few muscles. Moreover, a smile also increases our face value!

Vow for the third day:

Do some formal spiritual practices. Amma guarantees that in any household where the 1,000 names of Devi (the Goddess) are being chanted every day with devotion, the Divine Mother will always provide at least the minimal requirement of food and clothing. A beginner who finds the daily chanting of 1,000 Sanskrit names too difficult can try to spend at least an hour on weekends in remembrance of God: in chanting, mantra japa, puja, meditation, bhajans, etc.

Vow for the fourth day:

Don't give in to a bad habit. A habitual smoker or someone addicted to drugs or drinking may find it difficult to abandon the bad habit completely despite his or her best efforts. Try to abstain from the habit on Thursdays, for example, as obeisance to the Guru, since Thursday is considered the Guru's day. Slowly, as you gain more and more control over the mind, it will become easier to get rid of any deep-rooted bad habits at will. Though you may be free from addictive habits such as smoking, drinking or using drugs, you can train your mind by abstaining for just one day a week from some other item to which you are attached. Attachments might include a favorite food or television program. Amma says spirituality is the ability to stop the flow of the mind anytime, at will, like applying the brakes of a new, well-made car.

Vow for the fifth day:

Reduce food. When you rest physically, the body is allowed to rest, but the stomach will continue to work hard, digesting the food you have eaten. If once a week you take only one meal on that day, it will give your digestive system a rest from its ceaseless work and is therefore good for your health. On that day, you should drink sufficient water. Sick people who are advised by their doctors not to fast need not observe this vow of one meal a day. They might consider adopting a different austerity.

Vow for the sixth day:

Be helpful. There are many vistas of selfless service. If you are paying attention, you can always find an opportunity to serve others. If you are unable to find a way to serve others directly, you can share a portion of your income with one or several organizations engaged in social service. The best form of selfless service is where no one (including the beneficiary) is aware of who is giving the help.

Vow for the seventh day:

Observe silence. Though it may be difficult to keep a vow of absolute silence for the entire day, you can start with one hour, beginning from the time you wake up. The following week you can try to increase it to two hours or more, and slowly work your way up to a full day. If your responsibilities do not permit you to keep silence for the whole day, then speak only when it is really necessary. Do not gossip or engage in meaningless conversation. Amma says that excessive talking increases mental turbulence, drains one's energy and drowns the subtle voice of God within. When we observe silence, even though thoughts continue to arise, we are conserving energy that will help us to focus our minds on God. Amma says that thoughts can be compared to ripples on the surface of a glass of water—though the surface is disturbed, no water is lost. But when we speak, it is like water overflowing or being spilled.

Once a month, reflect on both the progress you are making and the progress you still want to make, and see if it is time to change the focus of any of the vows. Amma says that every spiritual aspirant needs to cultivate patience, enthusiasm, and optimistic faith. Encourage yourself to keep trying.

All that Amma asks is that we surrender our negative habits and flaws at Her lotus feet, and in return, take one or two of the countless divine qualities from Amma as Her prasad. These vows are the lamp that will light the way during our journey through the dark forest of ignorance and also save others from going astray. One can follow at least some of these vows without much difficulty.

If we are able to cultivate at least one good habit, many other good habits will follow in its wake. If one ant goes somewhere, other ants will follow. Likewise, one good habit is enough to make other habits follow suit.

There is a verse in the *Bhagavad Gita* in which Lord Krishna says that no effort on the spiritual path ever goes in vain, nor can it bring any harm. Even a little of this dharma of cultivating good values and good habits in our lives will have a beneficial result.

DEDICATING OUR ACTIONS
TO THE GURU OR GOD

If we are able to develop the strong conviction that that our Guru is one with God, and whatever He or She advises us is only for our own benefit, we will able to cultivate love and dedication toward our Guru. Gradually we will want to dedicate all our actions to Him or Her. This is the best way of worshipping Amma. We need not ask if we can perform a negative action and dedicate it to Amma. If we love Amma so much that we want to dedicate all our actions to Her, it will be difficult for us to perform any harmful actions. Of course, the same is true for dedicating our actions to God. By dedicating our actions to the Guru or God, we can begin to reduce our negative actions and finally eliminate them entirely. By lovingly dedicating our day-to-day activities to Amma or God, we purify all our actions.

Even if we aren't able to dedicate all our actions to God, simply doing our duty sincerely will bring us merit. The scriptures declare that it is meritorious to do our duty sincerely.

THE MAHATMA'S ROLE
IN RESTORING HARMONY

All living bodies have an immune system, which prevents foreign objects from entering and staying in the body. For example, if an insect or a piece of dirt enters the eye, tears will immediately flow and push the foreign object to one corner of the eye. If something irritates the nose, such as pollen or chili powder, we will immediately sneeze. When germs invade the body, the immune system fights to eliminate them. Mahatmas like Amma are the "immune system" of humanity, protecting the planet from infections of unrighteousness, crime, violence, anger, and hatred. Amma says that Mahatmas are like the pillars of a building. The pillars provide the real support for a building. Likewise, Mahatmas with their unconditional love, compassion and pure vibrations support the Creation in many ways.

One finds that most of the gods and goddesses in Hindu mythology are armed with various weapons. This has caused many westerners to think that these deities represent despotic and often demonic forces, and that people worship them out of fear and ignorance. This is not true. The weapons are often symbolic. For instance, the sword of Kali symbolizes the power of discrimination and the trident represents the three basic qualities of serenity, activity and rest. These weapons are used to destroy unrighteousness. Avatars like Rama and Krishna always tried to transform the wicked through reason, diplomacy and charity. Only when they failed in all three modes of peaceful approach did they use the only avenue left open to them—to punish or kill the wrongdoer. It was their duty to do so because they were responsible for maintaining dharma in the nation.

While Rama and Krishna killed the wicked people who refused to reform their ways, Amma is killing the wicked qualities in us. She is cleaning our minds and thus changing our behavior.

The purpose of all Avatars is to restore the harmony of the world. The methods they use to accomplish this goal differ in accordance with the customs, systems, and circumstances prevailing at the time. If an object falls into our eye, sneezing won't help. If a fly enters the nose, tears won't help. Depending on the prevailing situation, the Avatars and Mahatmas will adopt different means and methods to re-establish dharma.

AMMA'S WEAPON

Rama's weapon was a bow and arrow. Krishna's weapon was a discus. Amma uses the weapon of Love. Of course Rama and Krishna were also embodiments of supreme love, but as Rama was a king and Krishna was an advisor and friend to kings, it was their dharma to take up arms against adharmic forces. But as Amma has come to the world as the Universal Mother, Her main weapon is Love.

With infinite love and patience, Amma sits with us hour after hour, listening to our problems, consoling us and giving us the strength we need to face our challenges. It is the power of love that makes so many people want to join Amma's army of selfless service. The power of love transcends nationality, religion, language, culture— everything. Amma's love helps us to transform and remove our negativities.

We all have love of power, but we have no power of love. Ours is a selfish love. Amma's love is beyond all earthly love. It is the power of Amma's love that makes us forget our worries. Amma comes down to our level, sings with us, dances with us, jokes with us and sheds tears with us in order to help us to attune ourselves to Her and rise up to Her level.

There was a crazy person staying at the ashram for a few years. No one wanted to talk to him because whatever he said did not make much sense. But whenever he came for darshan Amma spent extra time with him, asking him things like, "Are you happy, my son? Do you get enough food?" One day Amma asked him, "Why do you look so sad?"

He replied, "I am not only sad—I'm angry with You, Amma, because You didn't give me much attention the last time I came for darshan!" If we were in Her position, we would have simply brushed him aside. But Amma spent almost ten minutes explaining to him how much She cares for him and how it was because of the crowd that She had not been able to give him enough attention that day. After hearing Amma's words, he felt so happy.

In the early days of the ashram, there were many atheists and troublemakers who would abuse and criticize Amma. Being the very embodiment of patience and love, She bore this ill treatment without being disturbed in any way and without reacting. However, when the miscreants harassed any of Her devotees, She was deeply concerned. Amma explains Her own nature with the help of a comparison: "If the base of a tree is pricked, it doesn't matter—but if a tender branch of that tree is pricked, it affects the tree."

I remember one particular time when Amma was giving darshan in Krishna Bhava. As usual, a pleasant and enchanting smile lit up Her face, and the devotees were immersed in the bliss of Her divine presence. At that moment a devotee entered the temple completely distraught. He had been severely harassed by some local atheists. Deeply upset and agitated, he fell at Amma's feet, sobbing uncontrollably. He appealed to Amma to find some remedy for the situation. Suddenly Amma's facial expression changed and She looked extremely fierce. Her eyes seemed like two smoldering iron balls, emitting shooting flames of anger all around.

She joined Her fingers in the Devi mudra. This was the first time that Amma assumed the fierce aspect of the Goddess. Only after much prayer and chanting of various mantras did She become calm. Amma later explained, "Seeing the distress of that devotee, I felt like destroying all the unrighteous people who persist in harassing the devotees. Spontaneously, the fierce aspect of the Divine Mother manifested to grant refuge to the persecuted."

CHAPTER 12

THE POWER OF LOVE

LOVE ONLY GIVES

There are many different kinds of power, but most are limited in scope. There are activities in which muscle power is necessary, such as lifting heavy objects or running a marathon. However, the value of that sort of power is limited. For example, the physical strength of a person is totally useless in pacifying a crying baby. Monetary power is also limited. If you are bereaved because a loved one has died, no amount of money can remove your sorrow. Political power, too, has its limitations.

However, no one has yet discovered the boundaries of the power of love. Love is the bridge that unites humanity with divinity. We all know that God is limitless and all-powerful. And we know that God is love. Therefore, the power of love must also be limitless. Love is expressed in giving. Love never takes anything. Love is always on the lookout for opportunities to give.

LOVE TRANSFORMS

Amma always says that love is the foundation of life. Where there is real love, there will be fewer problems, and where there is less love, there will be more problems. All problems can be resolved through love.

We may think that this perspective is only the wishful thinking of a loving mother and cannot be true in daily life. If love can solve all problems, then why is there so much bloodshed and violence on this beautiful earth?

We usually resort to force and violence to achieve our goals because we do not have enough patience, understanding and perseverance. If we are armed with pure love and if we can express that love in our every thought, word and deed, then we can wipe out the blemish of war and violence from the face of the earth.

In Amma's speech at the Millennium World Peace Summit at the United Nations, She said, "What cannot be accomplished with force, violence, and war can be accomplished with love."

What Amma has accomplished with Her love stands as the best example of the truth of this statement. Though She was treated harshly by many of the villagers during Her childhood and teens, She never reacted to their cruelties with any hatred or resentment. Just as a fruit tree provides sweet fruits even when stones are thrown at it, Amma responded to the villagers' hostility and hatred with Her magnanimous charitable projects that She continues to provide even today.

When Amma returned home after the UN summit, She received a touching reception from those same villagers who had been so hostile and hateful toward Her for so many years. The same hands that once threw stones at

Amma and committed many malicious acts against the ashram, now offered flower petals on Her path. The same tongues that once abused and tried to dishonor Amma were now chanting the mantra, "Om Amriteswaryai Namah," which means, "Salutations to the Divine Mother Amritanandamayi."

It took almost five hours for Amma to travel a distance of eight miles to reach the ashram from the main road because of the gatherings along Her route. All the families lit oil lamps in front of their homes as a sign of respect and reverence, and they waited at their doorsteps for hours to receive a passing glance from Amma. As soon as Amma reached the ashram, it started drizzling; it seemed as though Mother Nature herself was shedding tears of joy seeing the tremendous change in the attitude of the villagers. This is the miracle of love. Amma's life is an unending series of such miracles.

AMMA BREAKS AN ASHRAM RULE

Two hurdles to my becoming a sannyasi were my attachment to my parents and my love for yogurt and buttermilk. I was very attached to my parents. I never thought I would leave them to stay in an ashram. Also, I was used to eating yogurt or buttermilk every day with my food and couldn't imagine relishing the ashram food day after day without these items. At that time, yogurt and buttermilk were not served in the ashram—definitely not for brahmacharis! Eating rich yogurt every day is not considered conducive to maintaining celibacy. Also, yogurt was not a regular part of the diet in the area surrounding the ashram.

However, in my case, when Amma asked me whether I would like to stay at the ashram as a brahmachari, I responded, "It's all right if I can still have yogurt and buttermilk like I get in my house."

Amma said, "That won't be a problem." And She made a special arrangement to supply yogurt for me. Amma's love does not mind breaking any rule or custom to save a soul. She knew very well that if I stayed out of the protective atmosphere of the ashram, the chances were high that I would be caught up by illusory sense pleasures.

My mother once wrote me a letter abusing Amma and calling Her a fisherwoman. This made me very angry. Because I had experienced Amma's selfless love and Her spiritual glory, I could not stand Amma being criticized or abused. In retaliation, I decided that I would not visit my parents until they apologized or wrote something good about Amma.

They did neither. Instead, they hired a priest to perform tantric[8] rites to make me change my mind so that I would leave the ashram and come back home. They also sent me a talisman (pendant) to wear around my neck. The talisman had been energized by the chanting of some powerful

---

[8] *Tantra* is a system of worship to gain the blessings of a higher power. Emphasis is placed on *mudras* rather than mantras.

mantras. They sent it through one of my relatives who wouldn't leave the ashram unless I put it around my neck. Finally, I took the matter to Amma, and Amma said, "Even though it is powerful enough to unsettle and disturb you, don't worry. Just wear it. Amma will protect you so that it doesn't harm you." She wanted me to wear it just to satisfy my parents, so I tied it around my neck. Even though my parents were completely against Amma, She was exceedingly loving toward them and never missed an opportunity to please them.

My parents had expected me to change my decision and come back home soon, because the priest who had performed the tantric ritual to change my mind was very famous for being an expert in these procedures. They were surprised to see that there was no change in my attitude, and they then realized that Amma must be a more powerful person than they had thought, since the priest's rituals and incantations didn't work with Her.

Over a period of time, many incidents convinced them that Amma is one with the Divine Mother, whom they worshipped every day. That brought about a great transformation in their life, and eventually they became devotees of Amma.

NOT THE QUANTITY, BUT THE QUALITY

Many years ago, a female devotee from Tamil Nadu came to see Amma for the first time. As I speak Tamil, I acted as her translator. She was deeply impressed by

Amma's love and spiritual energy, and before She went back home, She made a generous donation to the ashram. At the time we were in a pitiful financial situation, so this was really a boon, a fortune for the ashram.

A month later, She again visited the ashram. When She arrived, Amma had just finished giving darshan and had returned to Her room. When I saw the woman, I went running to Amma's room, thinking, "Amma will be very impressed and will immediately come down and talk to the lady, because the last time this woman visited the ashram, she made a big donation." I knocked on the door to Amma's room, and the door opened. Amma was reading letters written by the devotees. She asked me, "What's the matter?" From the look on Her face, I knew that I had displeased Her. I hesitated to speak, but still I mustered some courage and said, "That lady from Tamil Nadu, who made a big donation last month, has come."

Amma asked, "So what? What should I do?"

I didn't know what to say. I mumbled a few words and then returned to my room. I didn't even go to meet the lady. After some time Amma came out and stood on the balcony of Her room. I happened to go by that way for some other reason. She called me asking, "Are there any devotees waiting to see me?" I immediately seized the opportunity, "Yes, yes, Amma. That lady from Tamil Nadu is waiting."

"Stop it!" She said. "I didn't ask about that lady. Is there anyone else waiting there?"

I told Amma I would find out and went to look. I saw a husband, wife and their children. From just looking at them, I could tell that they were from a very poor family. The children had runny noses, dirty cheeks and unkempt hair. Anybody would have taken them for beggars. It turned out that when they arrived at the ashram, they discovered that the darshan was over and that they could not see Amma. They were so upset by this that they started crying. It was at this time that Amma sent me to see if anyone was waiting to see Her.

I went back to Amma immediately and said, "Amma, there is a family waiting. They came to see you, but since you had already gone, they were not able to have your darshan. They have to return home today. They said that they run a small teashop." They had closed the teashop and come to the ashram to see Amma. If they did not return home by evening, they wouldn't be able to open the teashop the next day, their only means of livelihood. Amma immediately asked me to bring them to Her room. I was surprised. On the one hand, this wealthy and generous lady was waiting to see Amma, and Amma would not see Her. On the other hand, Amma was calling this poor family to Her room! Amma talked to them and consoled them. Amma spent nearly half an hour with them and gave them prasad.

I could not control my curiosity. I asked, "Amma, I would like to understand why You acted as You did today. That poor family that you met now is going to be of no help to the ashram, whereas the rich lady waiting to see you can be of great help to our ashram in many ways."

Amma immediately replied in a very serious tone that She is not doing Her work expecting any help from anyone, although She is always ready to help anyone in need. She said, "That poor couple comes to the ashram every week. They run a very small teashop and are barely able to make ends meet. Whatever they make, they accept happily. Their only income comes from selling tea and snacks in their little shop. They are so poor that it is only with the money they make each day that they can buy rice and food for the next day. One day a week the husband and wife fast and come to see Amma with the money they would otherwise have spent on food. Last week, they had a few rupees extra, and they offered this as a donation."

The wealthy lady had given a large donation, but Amma didn't give her any special attention. Compared to that huge donation, what the poor family donated was nothing. But considering how poor this family was, Amma said that their donation was priceless.

It should be mentioned that later, Amma did call the wealthy lady to Her room, and spent some time with her.

CHAPTER 13

RENUNCIATION

THE GIFT THAT AMMA CHERISHES

During one of Amma's birthday celebrations a few years ago, a group of college students came with a large, neatly wrapped box. They presented it to Amma, saying that it was their birthday gift to Her. Amma smilingly accepted it, saying, "Namah Shivaya."

Then She told them, "This is a nice gift, but there is a better gift that you can give." They were youngsters and Amma knew they were in the habit of smoking cigarettes. So She said to them, "Children, countless people are suffering in this world. Many don't even have the money to buy a single painkiller, let alone medicines. If you give up smoking and save that money instead, you can use it to help at least a few of those suffering people each year.

"What do you gain by smoking? It only destroys your health and makes you a slave to a bad habit. You are sending out invitations to sickness and ill health and are paying the premium for an early death. It is even printed nowadays on each cigarette packet: 'Smoking is injurious to health. Smoking can cause cancer.' Even so, many are not able to give up the habit of smoking. Some people even think of smoking as a status symbol. The real and lasting status comes from an expansive mind and not from such harmful habits.

"If you can give up, or at least reduce smoking, and use the money thus saved to help the poor, Amma would consider that as the best gift you could possibly give Her." The youngsters became pensive for a while. They were well aware of the power of addiction to smoking and how difficult it was to break the habit. So they said, "We'll try, but we need your blessings and grace."

Amma responded, "If you can't stop, then bring me all the cigarette butts from the cigarettes you have smoked. The thought that the cigarette butt will be given to Amma will help you to a great extent not to smoke." Amma sent them off with those words.

On the eve of the next birthday, they came with two gift packets colorfully wrapped and sealed. They insisted that Amma should open the packets and see then and there what was inside. Amma opened the first box, while the students beamed triumphantly. "This is the dearest gift you could give Amma," Amma exclaimed with loud laughter. Everybody leaned forward to take a look at the gift that was so cherished by Amma. The box was empty! No cigarette butts, which meant that none of them had smoked even a single cigarette the entire year, since they had promised Amma they would try. In the second box there were some clothes, some notebooks, and some pens and pencils for the students in the orphanage. Those teenagers had successfully kept their promise to Amma.

We, too, can try to give Amma this type of gift—the gift of renunciation and sacrifice. She doesn't want any material things from us. She wants Her children to help the poor and the suffering at least to a small extent, by giving up some of our addictions and luxuries. The motto on the emblem of Amma's ashram (*tyagenaike amritatwamanasuh*) means, "Without renunciation, Truth cannot be realized." This forms part of a hymn from the Upanishads, which says, "Not by actions, nor by progeny, nor by wealth or money, but through renunciation alone is immortality attained."

THE TRUE SPIRIT OF RENUNCIATION

When we talk about renunciation, we may immediately think that we must give up our family, our wealth, our house and all other possessions, and spend all our time in meditation. This is not so. Renunciation means giving up attachment to our possessions. In Sanskrit this attachment is called *mamakara,* which means "the sense of ownership or mine-ness." It is the twin of *ahamkara* (ego). Breaking the sense of limitation imposed by the feeling of I and mine and by the ego is called liberation or *moksha* in the philosophy of Vedanta.

When I think that this amount of land is mine, I am saying that the rest of the land, the earth, is not related to me. In this way I am imposing a limitation on the infinite nature of my true Self. Similarly, when I think that I am this body, mind and intellect, I am allowing only a rela-

tively tiny image of myself and forgetting that I am one
with the all-pervading Consciousness.

It may be impractical to start practicing this universal
attitude immediately in all spheres of life as long as the ego
remains within us. The safe, practical way to liberation is
to link our life with the life of a Master who has realized
this unity of Self. Just as a boat chained to a ship can cross
the ocean without any effort of its own, by linking our life
with that of a Master, we also can reach the other shore of
this ocean of life and death.

We each came to this world alone, and no one is going
to go with us when we leave. This body, our birthplace and
our parents were not consciously chosen by us. This being
the case, we should also be ready to accept that everything
we hold dear in this life, all our relatives and friends and all
our accomplishments are also gifts from the Almighty. We
love and value these gifts, but how often do we remember
God who gave us all these things?

When we understand that this life itself is a gift from
God, then we have the attitude of heartfelt thankfulness to
God and the Creation that is God's expression. The
Master's presence and life teaches us this truth. The
Master, being one with God, gives us a focal point on
which to develop our love and dedication to God. If we
have the attitude that whatever comes to us is given to us
by Amma, and that whatever we lose is our offering to Her,
then we will have equanimity of mind in all circumstances.
This is true renunciation.

Renunciation does not necessarily mean giving up everything and going to an ashram, or that we shouldn't love our children or marriage partner. We can live with our family with a spirit of detachment. We should do everything as our duty, but at the same time we need to remember that everything will vanish one day, at the time of death. We should be prepared for that. This is the real attitude of renunciation.

Janaka was a very famous king in ancient India. He was a real jnani, one who had realized the Truth. King Janaka had a Guru whose name was Yagnayavalkya. Even though Janaka was a king, he attended the scriptural classes along with Yagnayavalkya's many other disciples. The Guru greatly loved King Janaka for his deep spirituality and granted him certain privileges. Sometimes the Guru would wait to begin the class if King Janaka hadn't yet arrived, but if the other disciples came late, he didn't wait for them. And, even if the other disciples weren't there and King Janaka had arrived early, the Guru would immediately begin the class. The other disciples didn't understand this and were jealous. They thought the Guru was partial because Janaka was a wealthy king, and they concluded that the Guru's attitude was not correct. Some rumormongers spread this idea among others as well. There was a general unrest among the students.

However, understanding their mental attitude, Yagnayavalkya wanted them to see the error of their hasty conclusions. He created an illusion of fire with his great spiritual power.

In the midst of the class, a messenger from King Janaka's palace arrived in a great hurry, and after receiving the Guru's permission, gave Janaka a note and whispered something in his ear. The other disciples saw this, and one of them who was sitting next to Janaka peeped at the note to find out what it was all about. The Guru stopped the class for a while and closed his eyes. When he opened his eyes, no one but Janaka remained in the classroom. All the other disciples had run off. He continued the class with only Janaka sitting there, serene and calm.

After some time, the disciples came back and found that the class was already over. They became angry with the Guru and asked, "Why did you finish the class so soon? No one was here. You should have waited for us to return."

The Guru replied, "Janaka was here." They became even angrier and said to the Guru, "Don't you know what happened?"

"No, what happened?" asked the Guru innocently.

"The royal palace caught fire," they replied.

The Guru responded, "So what? You don't live in the palace. Why should it bother you?"

"We had hung our loincloths to dry near the compound wall of the palace. They would have been burnt. It was really God's grace that we were able to get there in the nick of time!"

The Guru turned to Janaka and asked, "Didn't you know that the palace was on fire? Isn't it your duty to save it? What were you doing here, sitting so quietly?"

With great humility, Janaka replied, "Master, life is uncertain. Who knows whether I will take the next breath? Before death takes away the body, one has to realize the immortality of the Self. Then one can save not only oneself but the whole of humanity. At the feet of a great Master like you, Self-realization can take place at any moment. Only a fool will miss a golden opportunity to listen to the teachings of his Guru in order to try to safeguard things that are perishable by their very nature."

To show his disciples the greatness of King Janaka, Yagnayavalkya said to them, "Janaka is the king of the whole country. The palace is his home, and even though he knew it had caught fire, he still did not move from here. He is not at all attached to valuable possessions though he lives in their midst, while you have just a few petty possessions like your loincloths, and yet you are so attached to them. You will try to save them even at the cost of Self-realization. One may be a sannyasi, and yet be attached to small, petty things like a begging bowl, a pair of sandals or a walking stick. On the other hand, there are people who have many children and many responsibilities, and yet they are totally detached. This mental attitude is true renunciation."

MANY OPPORTUNITIES TO PRACTICE RENUNCIATION

Suppose we sleep eight hours a night. Why don't we reduce it by half an hour? Make the commitment, "From now on, I will sleep only seven and a half hours." That is renunciation. Suppose we are eating four times a day. We can decide, "I will eat only three times a day, without increasing the quantity of food I am currently eating at each meal."

The mind doesn't want to be disciplined. An undisciplined mind will generally be agitated and restless. Otherwise, we would be happy and peaceful like Amma. Whenever we try to enforce some discipline, there is an inner struggle, but we must not give up the effort. If we are able to discipline our minds, we can realize God.

Many of us don't want to meditate for a long time. We may not like to do yogasanas for a long time either. However, when we persist in these spiritual practices as a discipline, we are practicing renunciation indirectly. Even though we want to get up after half an hour of meditation, if we make a strong determination that today we will sit for 45 minutes, that is renunciation (i.e. renunciation of our strong desire to get up after 30 minutes). There are many opportunities for us to practice such acts of renunciation in our daily life. In this way our mind can be trained.

Many people think they can turn to spirituality once they have earned enough money, attained the position they want and enjoyed all sense pleasures they could possibly want. Only then do they wish to consider renunciation. This is never going to happen. Our mind and body will not obey us even if we do manage to start praying and meditating when we are old. It will be much more difficult to control our mind, to reduce our thoughts, and to keep our body still for a long time when we are old. So it is always better to start our spiritual quest at an early age—the earlier, the better.

FAMILIAR FACES OF RENUNCIATION

Renunciation is not something new to us. We frequently practice it in our day-to-day lives, but usually only for selfish purposes. Amma gives an example of this type of renunciation. Many people claim they don't have time to go for satsang or to a temple or a church for worship, yet they can be found waiting for hours in a hospital if their son or daughter is sick. In the hospital they may have to undergo many discomforts, but they endure these experiences without complaint. This is a type of renunciation performed for the sake of the family.

Amma also gives the following examples. When popular movies are shown in theaters in India, we can see people standing in a long line exposed to the hot sun for several hours to get tickets. Such people don't mind these hardships. The same thing happens at the baseball park. People are so eager to get a ticket to see the game that they don't mind being pushed around by the crowd. These are different forms of renunciation, but they are of no lasting value.

Our present type of renunciation is like that of the boy renouncing his marbles when he is no longer interested in them. There were two brothers. One was five years old, and the other was eight. The eight-year-old snatched all the marbles from his younger brother and refused to give them back no matter how much the younger one cried. Every day, they fought over the marbles. This went on for quite some time.

One morning the older brother collected all the marbles from his drawer and gave them to the younger one. The little boy couldn't believe his eyes. He thought his brother must have gone crazy. Why else was he giving away those precious marbles? Was it, perhaps, that his brother had become generous overnight? The simple explanation was that their father had given the elder boy a bicycle, and he was no longer interested in the marbles. He didn't care about the marbles now that he had something much better.

Many people aren't eager for renunciation when it means serving others, doing spiritual practices or giving up some attachment. But the one time we do practice renunciation for a higher purpose is when we go to see Amma. Throughout the world, many people who do not normally forgo sleep, food and other comforts, wait for hours during Amma's darshan programs to experience a glimpse of Her divine love. When we are in Amma's presence, all of our petty concerns and attachments tend to fall away. Unfortunately, as soon as we go away from Amma, we are unable to sustain the same spirit.

Renunciation requires determination to change the direction or focus of our life from the worldly to the spiritual. We must be aware of the goal and be intent on reaching that goal.

THE GREATNESS OF TRUE SACRIFICE

The degree of our renunciation doesn't lie in the amount of money that we give in charity, nor in the value of the things that we renounce. It depends on the attitude and the context in which we perform the act of renunciation. There is a compelling story in the *Mahabharata* which exemplifies the essence of renunciation. After the great war, the Pandavas performed a grand sacrifice. During the sacrifice, they gave away cows, gold ornaments, money and other valuables to charity. The sacrifice lasted many days, and so much wealth and riches were distributed that everyone praised it as the greatest sacrifice ever performed. Though the Pandavas were virtuous by nature, they felt a little proud of their own magnanimity.

One day during the sacrifice, a mongoose came to the sacrificial ground. It was a strange mongoose, for one half of it was golden while the other half was brown like an ordinary mongoose. When the Pandavas saw this strange mongoose, they were curious.

To their surprise, the mongoose began to speak in a human voice and said, "The merits of the sacrifice you have performed are not even one percent of the merits acquired by the poor Brahmin family who gave in charity just a morsel of food." The Pandavas wanted to know more about his comments and inquired why his body was half golden. The mongoose replied, "Some years ago there was a Brahmin family in a country which was struck by famine and drought. There was no rain for many years, and all the crops withered away. The food stock dwindled, and people began to die of starvation. Many families were dying each day. This Brahmin family had managed to save a little bit of wheat flour. At last, that, too, was about to run out. So, they decided to fast for some days, and on the day that they felt they were going to die of starvation, they would use the flour to make a single chapatti to eat, so that they could survive for a few more days.

"They had fasted for many days; finally the day came that they felt they would die if they didn't eat. In this family there were four people: the husband and wife and their son and daughter-in-law. That day they decided to make a chapatti with the remaining flour, which they would split four ways. When they were about to eat, they saw a beggar standing in front of their house. He said, 'I have been starving for days. If you don't give me something to eat now, I will die, right in front of your house.' The husband felt very sad for him. He said, 'I am ready to give my share away, even if I die. I don't mind. At least I can save you. You are welcome to take my share.' The father gave his piece of the chapatti to the beggar, who gobbled it up.

"When we are hungry, if we get only a little food, it aggravates our hunger. This is what happened to the beggar. He was so hungry that he said, 'Oh, if you don't give me another piece, I will surely die.'

"Now the wife said, 'Right, I must follow my husband, so let me also give away my share.' She gave her share to the beggar, but still his hunger was not appeased. It was now the son's turn. The son also gave away his share. Still the beggar's hunger was not appeased.

"The son's wife then decided, 'Everybody has given away their share. Why, then, should I eat mine? Let me also give my share.' So she gave her share to the beggar. He ate it and left the place.

"Very soon, the whole family died of starvation. After they had died, I happened to go to their house hunting for some food. I found some wheat flour strewn here and there. When I rolled on the wheat flour, it stuck to one side of my body, and because of the greatness of the family's sacrifice, that side turned to gold. From that day on, I have visited all the places where people do charity, but I have found no place that could turn the other side of my body to gold. I had great expectations that by rolling in this holy place where this great sacrifice has been performed, the other half of my body would also turn to gold. Alas, my hopes have been betrayed."

The Brahmin family did not give a large amount of money to charity. Each member just gave a piece of chapatti. In those circumstances, it was the greatest sacrifice anyone could make. Whatever our position in life may be, whatever our background or situation, if we can practice renunciation, giving up something that we cherish most, some attachment we have, then that will be the greatest sacrifice.

CHAPTER 14

GOD'S GRACE

RIGHT EFFORT BRINGS GRACE

Most people have many aims and ambitions in life, but that alone is not enough. We need a concrete program to achieve our aims. There are certain elements that are essential to achieve any goal in life. Amma says, "No matter what our aims and ambitions are, to succeed we need three things: the right kind of effort, that the effort is made at the appropriate time, and God's grace."

Effort alone cannot bring about a positive result; God's grace must be present as well. Between our effort and the result, there are many other factors that influence the outcome, and many of these factors are not within our control. Although all factors have to be favorable for us to obtain the desired result, we cannot change or impact the factors that are beyond our control. Only God's grace can make those factors favorable and give us positive results for our effort.

Grace is not something that we receive on demand. Amma always says that grace has to be earned, which implies that there has to be some effort. We have to put forth effort sincerely and wait patiently for grace.

It is here that Mahatmas and Satgurus play a vital role. The grace that we receive from Mahatmas and Satgurus like Amma is not different from God's grace. Mahatmas and Satgurus are embodiments of unconditional love and compassion. Their only purpose is to help us to emerge from worldly problems and bondages and to take us to God or the Truth.

Amma says that the period during which such Mahatmas and great Masters live in this world is like a holiday sale. During certain times in a year, for example around Christmas, Deepavali and Ramadan, clothes, furniture and other things are available at a reduced price. If we buy these items during a sale season, we pay less than at other times. Similarly, the periods during which Mahatmas live can be likened to a sale season of grace. Through their grace, we can gain the desired result with less effort on our part than would otherwise be required. This benefit is true not only in accomplishing our goals, but also in overcoming difficult situations.

Spirituality is not confined simply to sitting and meditating; it also includes the way we talk to others, how we behave toward other people, etc. If we don't make the right effort, praying, "Give me grace, give me grace," will not yield a result.

Amma tells a very funny story about lack of effort. There was a poor man who prayed to God every day. One day an idea came to him. He thought, "I want to be rich. If God blesses me, surely I will be rich in no time. So why don't I pray for that?" From then on, he prayed to God,

"Oh, Lord, please make me rich!" After a few days, not having found any change in his financial position, he thought, "Perhaps I should pray to get money in a specific way." In his city they had a monthly lottery. So he prayed, "O Lord, with your grace, let me win first prize in the lottery this month!" When the lottery was drawn, he didn't even win the last prize, let alone the first prize. He was rather disappointed, but he thought, "Next month there will be another drawing, so maybe I'll win that one."

When the next drawing came, he didn't win anything. He was getting upset but kept praying. Several months went by and still he didn't win any money. One day he became very angry and started shouting at God, "Lord, why don't you hear me? Can't you answer my simple prayers?"

Suddenly, he heard God's voice, "My son, of course I know your problems and can hear your prayers, and I am very eager to help you."

The man became even angrier. "If so, why this delay? Why can't you make me win the first prize in the lottery?"

God replied, "I am waiting to help you, my child, but what can I do if you don't buy a single lottery ticket?"

Likewise, if we simply keep praying, "O Lord, please give me your grace," it's not going to work. We always pray for grace, but we don't always put forth the positive effort required. Without God's grace, our effort cannot bear fruit, but without our effort, God's grace is impeded.

God's grace or the Guru's grace can also mitigate our negative karma. Once, some of the brahmacharis went with

Amma to hold a program in Kottayam, a city some distance from the ashram. On the way back, we visited a house in a small village at the request of the devotees living there. Amma conducted a puja in their house, and after the puja She spent some time talking with the family. They were overjoyed to have Amma visit their home. At one point Amma became introverted, and the room fell silent. Suddenly, Amma got up and walked out the back door without a word of explanation. It was already three or four in the morning and pitch black outside. The father of the house rushed to bring Her a flashlight to light Her way, but by the time he brought it, She was already out walking through the mango grove in the backyard. As he didn't want to disturb Her, he followed at a slight distance and shone the light at Her feet.

Amma returned to the house about ten minutes later. Right away everyone noticed that one of Her toes was bleeding; She must have cut Her foot while walking in the dark. The family was very upset and did everything they could to clean and dress the wound properly. Then the brahmacharis accompanied Amma back to the ashram.

One day, a few months later, this family came to visit Amma at the ashram. They told Amma that the village where they lived had been robbed; a gang of criminals had gone from house to house, robbing, severely beating, and even killing a few of the residents who resisted. This family's house had been robbed, but no one in the house had been hurt. The family knew it was due to Amma's grace that they had not been attacked, and they came to the ashram to express their gratitude to Her. When they told Amma about this incident, I heard Her comment, "I already spilled blood in your house. That is why no one was hurt there." Amma didn't explain further, but when I heard Her say this, I understood that blood was destined to be spilled in that house. By receiving the wound on Her foot and bleeding in their home, Amma had protected the family from the harm that had been destined to befall them.

FROM SELFISHNESS TO SELFLESSNESS

A wonderful advantage of coming to a Mahatma is that the great Masters shower their grace upon us, without first demanding any qualifications from us. They help us to achieve our goal with less effort than might have been required otherwise.

Amma gives the example of a sailboat. If we travel in a sailboat during a favorable wind, we just have to set the sail to catch the wind, and the journey will be fast and easy. We don't need to row the boat with all our strength because the wind pushes the boat forward. Similarly, when a Mahatma like Amma is living amongst us, the breeze of their grace and compassion is constantly blowing. We simply have to set our sails—open our hearts—to receive their grace.

Amma says that by being kind and loving and by self-lessly serving others, we can earn this grace. As much as our selfish activities prevent the inflow of grace, our self-less actions open up the gates for God's grace to flow to us.

Of course, we are all putting forth the maximum effort in our worldly pursuits—getting a good job, making money, attaining a high status in society—but these efforts are mostly selfish in nature. Most of the time we don't do anything selflessly; yet we take endlessly from nature and society. The harmony among human beings, animals, plants and natural forces is disrupted by our selfishness. Our selfishness is the only dissonant note in the grand symphony of life on earth.

Those who continuously take from the world are leading the most selfish kind of life. Such a person is called a thief by Lord Krishna in the *Bhagavad Gita*. The selfishness of a person is harmful to nature and to everyone, including him- or herself. Selfishness is like continuing to eat food but refusing to excrete. Abundance of wealth can diminish the life of a person just as much as stark poverty does.

At least a small amount of help should be given to others and to nature. We rarely bother to make any effort toward this end. We simply say, "God will take care of it." We don't want to give anything of ourselves. As long as we don't want to give to others, we are inhibiting the flow of God's grace toward us.

Amma says that if we are doing everything for our own sake twenty-four hours a day, we should at least try to spend some time praying for the peace and welfare of other beings. Whenever there is an opportunity for us to help others physically, with our talents, financially, or in any other way, it is always good to do so.

Amma often talks about effort and grace. God's grace is the most important element in getting the desired results of our efforts. Amma gives the example of two candidates who are appearing for an interview for a single post. Both of them have the same qualifications, and both of them answer the questions correctly during the interview. Which one of them is going to be selected? Only one will be chosen—the person who is able to gain the sympathy of the interviewer. What is it that helps one to generate this consideration in the heart of the other person? It is only God's grace. It is because of this grace that we sometimes see people who may not have fared well in an interview get through, whereas others who have answered the questions correctly are not selected.

In cricket matches, we can often see that when a batsman is about to score a century, he starts feeling nervous. In that situation, we can sometimes see even the worst fielders make a difficult catch when the batsman offers it, while at other times we can see even good fielders dropping a simple catch. Who can explain why this happens? Amma says it is grace that completes our efforts. We need to recognize that grace is a vitally important element in our lives.

Knowing that we need God's grace, it is also important to perform our actions at the appropriate time. Suppose you have a son who is very dear to you. You can't bear to see him cry or be sad at all. Then, when he is four or five years old, you have to send him to kindergarten. As you know, most children don't want to go to school. Many children will cry for several days until they get used to school. So, your son is also crying, and you are very upset about it because you cannot stand the sight of his tears. But even so, you won't think, "Maybe I should wait until he is fifteen years old. By that time he will know why he needs to go school and then he won't cry." Is that going to be a wise decision? Is postponing school going to help your child in any way? No one would wait until a child attains maturity to send him or her to kindergarten. We send our children to school at age five or six whether they cry or not. For we know from experience that the sorrow the child is experiencing now is only for his or her own good, and that the child should go to school at the proper age. Similarly, for every effort that we make in our lives, there is an appropriate time.

If we sow seeds off-season, for example during the monsoon, it will be difficult to get a good harvest because all the seeds will be washed away by the heavy rains. Then again, if God's grace is missing, we won't get the desired result even if we put forth all the required efforts at the appropriate time. For example, we may sow the seeds at the right time, take good care of the crops, and add just the right amount of manure and water—but if a flood or a cyclone occurs at harvest time, all our efforts will be wasted. So God's grace is the most important factor.

MASTERS AND AVATARS

When is the best time to invoke God's grace? The scriptures say it is when a God-realized Master is living amongst us. The Mahatmas have come to the world out of their overflowing compassion and only with the intention of helping us.

There is a story about why these Avatars come to this world. There was once a group of people traveling to another city. They were going through a dense forest. Unfortunately, the journey took longer than expected, and they soon ran out of food. For two or three days they kept on walking without any food. Finally, they came to a high wall of a compound. They wanted to know what was on the other side of the wall, so one of them climbed the wall to see. One of the others helped him up.

When he looked over the wall he exclaimed, "Oh, my goodness!" and jumped to the other side without saying anything to the others who were waiting to hear what he saw. The others kept waiting, thinking he would come back, but he didn't.

They sent a second person. He also said, "My goodness!" and jumped over the wall and never came back. So they asked a third person to go and describe what was on the other side. They pleaded with him not to do what the other two did. "Please come back and tell us what is there," they said, and then they helped him climb the wall. As he looked over the wall, he smiled and said, "Oh, it is incredible! It is marvelous! Just wait!" Having said this, he jumped over to the other side, but, like the others before him, he didn't come back either. He thought, "What's the hurry? Let me enjoy this for some time!"

What they found on the other side of the wall were beautiful fruit trees, a lovely spring and wonderful food to eat. They were so hungry they just jumped over and stuffed themselves until they couldn't move. So how could they climb back over the wall?

Before climbing the wall, the fourth person decided he would definitely come back. He jumped over, ate some food, and came back to tell the others about the delicious food, and he helped them climb over the wall so that they could enjoy the food as well.

It is said that the bliss of God-intoxication is so great that those who enjoy it never want to come back to the world, just as the first three persons who saw all the food and stuffed themselves never wanted to come back. A person like Amma makes a sankalpa: "I will not completely immerse myself in that bliss. I will come back. Countless people are suffering in the world, and others seek the Truth. I have to help them." So when they leave the body, they make a sankalpa to come back to the world to help and guide others toward that bliss. Amma has said many times that She is ready to take any number of births for the sake of Her children.

So we have to remember one important point: we are born because of our karma, but the birth of an Avatar like Amma happens only because of Her immense compassion for us.

There is the story of Dattan, the leper mentioned earlier in this book, who came to the ashram in the early days. Out of Her boundless compassion, Amma used to lick Dattan's wounds during Devi Bhava darshans. This was beyond any human being's comprehension. No one could even imagine doing such a thing. It is said that the saliva of a divine being has medicinal power. Still, if She had wanted to, Amma could have applied Her saliva on his wounds with Her fingers. But She didn't. Instead She licked those wounds. No one could even stand to watch it; it was such an awful sight. Some people who saw Amma do this fainted inside the temple. Some devotees simply walked out of the temple when Amma would give darshan to Dattan. Many people didn't want to get darshan from Amma after She had given darshan to Dattan for fear of getting infected with leprosy. You can see this scene in one of the videos of Amma's life. You have probably never before heard of anyone licking a leper's wounds, not even in stories. But here is a living example of that before us.

When I asked Amma, "How could you lick Dattan's wounds? Wasn't it disgusting?" the reply She gave astounded me.

She said, "It was just the spontaneous expression of My compassion toward him." Then Amma asked me, "If there happened to be an infected wound on your hand, what would you do? Would you cut off your hand?"

I said no.

"Why?" Amma asked.

"Because it's my hand," I said. "How could I cut off my own hand? I would try to heal it."

Then Amma said, "Likewise, I am not different from that leper. I am he. He is Me. In other words, I am in him and he is in Me."

This is why it is said that the Mahatmas have cosmic or universal consciousness. When Amma said that She is not different from Dattan, the leper, She was uttering the highest truth. A divine person is defined as a person who is able to see his or her own Self in everybody and everybody in his or her own Self. This is why Amma is able to be so compassionate and loving toward all beings.

A MASTER IS LIKE SPRING

When a Master like Amma is living amongst us and so readily available, it is easy to receive Her grace with a little bit of effort. Amma says, "If you take ten steps toward me, I am ready to take a hundred steps toward you. But you must at least take those ten steps!"

If we get something without any effort, we won't be able to appreciate its value. It will be wasted like gems given to small children. In Amma's eyes, everybody is equal. If we make a sincere effort, we will definitely receive Her grace.

The scriptures say, *"Brahmavid brahmaiva bavathi."* This means, "One who has realized Brahman becomes Brahman." This is one of the greatest statements of the

Upanishads. That is why it is said that whatever we receive from a God-realized person is actually coming from God.

On the other hand, whatever comes from us is the product of our likes and dislikes, our ego, etc. We can't claim that it comes from God. The Mahatmas are free from ego. They don't think of themselves as limited individuals. They are incapable of acting selfishly.

At present we cannot do this. We can love our own children but we don't necessarily love the neighbor's children. We love the members of our family, our friends, and our countrymen. It would be difficult for us to love others with that same passion and sincerity.

But the Mahatmas are always tuned to the Universal Consciousness and they can see that Consciousness in everything. This is so perfectly clear in Amma's life and Her words. When Amma gives darshan, we can see that She doesn't show any distinction between handsome and ugly, rich and poor, Indian and western. When She sees a handicapped or suffering person, we can see more of Her love and compassion being expressed, but that does not mean that She values such people more or less than others; it only shows that She is giving each person what he or she needs.

The great Adi Sankaracharya said that such Masters are like the spring season. In winter, especially in northern countries, it gets very cold; the sun sets early, bringing long nights; the trees look dead with all their leaves gone, and people tend to stay inside their houses. Even the birds don't sing much. In some parts of the world, the winter season is so long that the people become very depressed. And, then, after winter comes spring. When spring arrives, everything is given new life. Plants begin to grow and blossom. The trees grow new, fresh leaves, and the birds start singing happily. There is sunlight for a longer period of the day. People come out and are more active. Their depression lifts.

The great Masters are like springtime in that they bring joy to others through their presence, grace, unconditional love and compassion. Those who have spent time with Amma can perfectly relate to this fact. There is never a dull moment around Amma. Many people who come to Amma with a heavy heart, leave Her with a feeling of great relief, satisfaction and strength. Just as coolness is the nature of water and heat is the nature of fire, unconditional love and overflowing compassion are the nature of divine beings. They are also able to ignite the fire of love and compassion in the hearts of those who come into contact with them. Thus, they kindle feelings of love, joy and cheerfulness in those around them.

Most people feel as if they are being born again, as if life is made brand new when they come to Amma. Those who have been coming to see Amma and have lived with Amma can definitely vouch for this. It is such bliss to be in Amma's company; it is a rare fortune. Even if we don't meet all the requirements of good spiritual seekers, still, because of Amma's compassion, we are given more than we deserve.

If Amma were to look for qualifications to bless us, not many of us would receive Her blessings. Amma says that if She were to exclude some from Her love and blessings or discard those who are not good or pure, then it would be like building a super-specialty hospital and putting up a sign saying: "No sick people allowed!"

Although, many of us have experienced Amma's greatness numerous times, we tend to judge and evaluate Her according to our limited intellectual standards. Because Amma is in a human body like ours, we have a natural tendency to think of Her as an ordinary person. We may read wonderful stories and incidents about Amma, but we cannot comprehend who She really is.

Amma says Mahatmas are like huge icebergs. Only the tip of the iceberg is visible to us above the surface of water. Seeing this, a person may feel that he or she has seen and understood the great magnitude of the iceberg. But that person has seen only the tiniest fraction of the huge mass of ice which is submerged under the water. Likewise, we are able to perceive only an infinitesimal part of Amma's greatness. Much of Her greatness is hidden from us.

Amma tells a relevant story. There was a mouse in a forest. One day the mouse was running around frantically searching for something. As it ran, it came to a pond where a huge elephant was bathing. As soon as it saw the elephant, the mouse stopped and shouted, "Hey, elephant! Get out of the water!" At first the elephant didn't take any notice of the mouse; after all, an elephant is such an enormous animal and a mouse is a tiny creature. So the elephant pretended that he didn't hear the mouse, but the mouse was very persistent. He kept shouting, "Hey, elephant! Get out of the water!" Finally, reluctantly, the elephant came out of the water. No sooner had the elephant stepped out of the water than the mouse shouted, "That's enough. You can get back into the water now!"

The elephant was very annoyed. Angrily, he asked the mouse, "Then why did you ask me to come out?"

The mouse replied, "I have lost my swimming suit, and I just wanted to see if you were wearing it!"

The point of the story is that we can no more comprehend Amma with our limited intellect than an elephant could fit into the swimming suit of a mouse. Our intellectual capacity will never be sufficient for us to understand how great Amma is or who She is. We shouldn't underestimate Amma just because She has a human body and is so humble. Amma is not confined to the body.

A few years ago a group of devotees from Chennai were visiting the ashram. I was talking to them about Amma. Many devotees in the group were wondering how Amma could give darshan to so many people every day. I said to them that even though Amma has a human body like ours, She is actually beyond the body. I added that Amma is just using the human body to interact with us. One of the members of the group didn't agree with me on this point. He was not at all convinced. When he got a chance to talk to Amma, he asked, "Is it true that Mahatmas are beyond the body?"

Amma smiled and said, "Yes, it is true." But, even then he didn't seem convinced.

A little while later, the group from Tamil Nadu and some of the ashramites were sitting around Amma talking with Her. Suddenly this man exclaimed, "Where is Amma? What happened to Amma?"

We were surprised because we could clearly see Amma sitting right in front of us. We thought this person must be crazy. We asked him, "What's the matter? What are you talking about?"

He couldn't speak for some time. Finally, filled with wonder and amazement, he managed to explain that Amma's body had suddenly disappeared before his eyes, and in its place he had seen a mass of brilliant light. The light became brighter and brighter, blinding his eyes. Finally the light faded away and Amma's form reappeared. This experience convinced that man, who had been skeptical, that Amma is not the body.

This is the right time to put forth our effort and pray and work for Her grace. We should start our spiritual practices now, without wasting our time. Each second that has passed is lost forever. No amount of money or effort can bring it back.

I have heard a story highlighting the importance of not postponing our efforts. This story is about Karna, a king who was well known for his charity. Because he was so generous, he could never say no to a person who came seeking something from him. One night an old man came to Karna's palace asking for something. As Karna was eating at that time, the guards prevented the old man from entering. The old man was adamant and refused to leave unless he was allowed to meet the king. He said, "I know the king, and if he sees me, he'll definitely help me." Since there was no way to get rid of the old man, one of the guards went to Karna and told him the news.

Karna ordered the guard to bring him in immediately. Karna ordered another guard to bring from his treasury whatever that person wanted. When the guard came with some valuable jewels, Karna, who was eating with his right hand, took them with his left hand and gave them quickly to the old man. Some ministers were dining with the king, and when they saw Karna do this they wondered, "Why is the king acting in this fashion?"

One of the elders among them spoke up. "Your Majesty, what are you doing? If you are giving in charity, you must give it with the right hand. Moreover, this old man is a Brahmin."

In India it is the custom not to use the left hand to do good things. Indians as a rule use only the right hand (though there are some lefthanders), particularly when offering something to God, or giving something in charity, especially to a Brahmin. Karna said to the ministers, "You know, the mind is tricky. I don't know what my mind will think in the next moment. Now I feel I should help him. If I wait one minute to wash my hands, my mind may try to trick me saying, 'Why should I entertain or help this old man at this odd hour? Let him wait or come another day.' So I should not postpone it. I have to do it right now because the next moment is not in my control. I may breathe my last, or the other man may die, or my position as a king may be lost, or he may change his mind and go away. Anything can happen. That's why I gave it immediately."

Likewise, our minds are not under our control. Instead of our mind obeying us, we are obeying our mind. Whenever you feel like doing something good, do it immediately. If you postpone it, it might never happen. You can postpone bad things; there won't be any problem with that. In this context, Amma tells a funny story.

There was a very intelligent monkey that lived in a big tree near a temple. Many devotees would come to the temple, and from morning till evening they would sit under the tree and fast as a part of their worship. After watching this for some time, the monkey thought, "To please God, everybody is sitting under this tree without eating. So why can't I also do it? Perhaps God will bless me and I may become famous like Hanuman (the monkey god) whom even human beings worship." He thought about it for a few days and finally decided to start his fasting on an auspicious day. The day before that auspicious day, he reminded himself, "Tomorrow is fasting day; don't forget!"

As the night approached, he became a little afraid. He thought, "I have never fasted in my life. I'm used to eating something very often, and tomorrow I'll be fasting the whole day. I may get very tired and dizzy. Perhaps I won't even be able to walk. Unfortunately, there are no fruits in this tree, and to get fruit I would have to go a long distance." So he thought, "I may become so weak from my fasting that I won't be able to reach the fruit trees without fainting along the way. Maybe it would be best for me to stay near the fruit trees while I fast."

So he went and slept under a tree that had lots of fruit. In the middle of the night he woke with a start. "Tomorrow is my fasting day, and I'll be so tired when I'm done. What if I'm unable to climb the tree? This tree is really tall, and what if I fall down while climbing the tree to pluck the fruit, since I might be really tired and weak after my whole day fasting? I'd better climb up and sit on a branch, so that I won't have to go far to get some fruit."

Once he was there, he went back to sleep but again woke up with a start. "What if I am unable to even stretch out my arm? Let me pluck some fruit now and keep it in my lap." He picked some fruit and put it in his lap, but then the temptation was too much. He thought, "Now it is only dawn. By evening I will be so feeble due to fasting that I may not be able to lift the fruit to my mouth and chew it. How unfortunate it would be to die with ripe fruit in my lap. Also, it is not much distance between the lap and the stomach. So let me keep them in my stomach rather than keeping them on my lap. Perhaps I can fast on the next auspicious day. Let this day pass like the other days." Saying so, he gobbled up the fruit.

Needless to say, he was never able to fast.

Let us not be like the monkey in the story. We are all fortunate to have Amma with us. Without procrastinating, let us make every effort to progress on the spiritual path. Amma's presence will bring our practice swiftly to fruition. Because of Her humility, Amma may not say to each and every person, "I am here. If you make even a little effort on the spiritual path, I will give you quick results." Instead, indirectly She gives us a hint. She says: "Dig a well beside a river, and you will get water quickly."

CHAPTER 15

PURIFYING THE MIND

SACRIFICE, CHARITY AND PENANCE

In order to purify our minds and make life fruitful, the scriptures say we need to do three things every day. Lord Krishna classified them in the *Bhagavad Gita* as *yagna, danam* and *tapas*. The first category is yagna, or worship without expectation of personal gain. The second is danam (charity), which is to give away the things to which our mind is most attached. The third is tapas (penance), which is to make a conscious and continuous effort toward our spiritual upliftment. Lord Krishna also says that these actions should be performed without being attached to the results.

Yagna means worshipping or praying to God purely out of gratitude, without expecting any favor. After all, we owe our very life to God. To express our gratitude and indebtedness, Amma says we have to worship God. This can take different forms like chanting the 108 or 1000 names, chanting a mantra, meditating, singing bhajans or reading sacred texts.

Also, any collective selfless activity, either of service or worship, can be called a yagna. In olden days, great kings and rishis used to conduct various yagnas in which they would give away much of their wealth and wisdom in charity. When Amma conducts a collective puja, it is a modern version of a yagna.

Any collective service activity under a Master helps to eliminate our ego. Amma gives a pertinent example of how stones with sharp edges are put together in a machine and rotated so fast that the sharp edges of the stones are rounded off, and the stones become smooth and polished. Similarly, working together in an ashram gives many opportunities for our egos to rub against each other, and in that process get shaped and smoothed. That is the importance of staying in an ashram and doing seva in that environment, especially in the presence of a Master.

The second category is charity (danam). If you can afford it, you can help others financially. For example, if you know of any children who are not able to get an education for want of money, or if you know of any orphans or destitute people, you can help them financially. But Amma says that charity doesn't have to be given in the form of money. If you cannot extend financial help, you may have some skill or talent that can be used to help others. If you are physically strong, you can do some service in a temple, church, hospital or home for the elderly. According to the scriptures, giving wisdom as charity (*jnana danam*) is the highest form of charity because it will always remain with the receiver. If instead of giving money, we teach people how to make money, isn't that better? Thus, charity can take the form of our skills, talents, physical strength, money or knowledge.

What we give matters a great deal. It should be of some use to the receiver. Giving unusable things in the name of charity doesn't bring any merit to the donor. The attitude with which we give is also very important. The scriptures say, "When you give something to others, you should have a certain mental attitude. First of all, you should have a yearning to give even more, and without expecting anything in return. Secondly, you should be careful not to become egoistic or proud because you give. You should give with a feeling of modesty, with the attitude that the gift is meager and there are others who give even more. Finally, give with the knowledge that you are giving to your own Self, for there is only one all-pervading consciousness."

What better example do we need, with regard to the art of giving, than Amma? Amma always says She wants to help more and more people. Amma never takes pride in what She does, because to Her, we are all Her children—and a true mother doesn't take any pride in helping her children; She is only happy to do so. Thus, in Amma we see the most ideal attitude of giving.

Amma says that charity is a way of expressing our gratitude to God. We should be thankful to God for giving us opportunities to serve Him in various forms, and we shouldn't feel proud of our charitable deeds. If our services are not appreciated or praised, we shouldn't feel that people are ungrateful or that they are not giving us our due honor. Such an attitude won't help our spiritual growth.

Our intention should be only to help others as far as possible, whether the recipients appear grateful or not.

The third category is tapas (penance). In olden days, people did severe tapas, such as standing on one leg for hours or even days on end, sitting out in the rain and sun for many days, sitting on a bed of thorns or fasting for days on end. These austerities would be performed in order to gain occult powers, overcome physical limitations, master the mind or get the vision of God. These days, tapas of the above mentioned types are unthinkable because no one has the temperament to do that kind of tapas. Even doing simple kinds of spiritual practices like meditating regularly in the morning or evening, or chanting the 1000 Names of the Divine Mother every day is a kind of tapas because of the pace of modern life and our dependence on so many objects and gadgets.

The word *tapas* literally means "creating heat." Spiritual practices that create heat due to the friction of opposing forces within the mind can be called tapas. Striving toward something good is also tapas. Cultivating good habits like controlling anger, being patient, not judging others and not finding fault with others involves a lot of internal struggle. This is because we are not used to practicing such positive qualities, and at the same time we have allowed the negative qualities to thrive and grow as much as they wanted. Now that we want to undo them, naturally there will be a great struggle.

There was once a man who had the habit of drinking coffee at seven o'clock in the morning and meditating after that. One day his wife happened to think she had already given her husband his morning coffee, so she got busy with the other household chores. The husband kept waiting for his coffee. He was rather upset. He postponed his meditation and waited for his coffee till 7:30, then till 8:00, and then till 8:30, but his wife never brought it. Finally it was time for him to leave for his office. Thus, he missed his meditation. Instead of waiting for his wife to bring him his coffee, he could have made the coffee himself! Or why couldn't he have meditated and then drunk the coffee? Instead of waiting for the coffee to arrive, he could have started his meditation—but, then, his meditation shouldn't be on coffee! I am sure that doing something other than the usual (waiting for his wife to serve him) would have been a struggle indeed. That was a chance for practicing the spirit of tapas, but he missed it.

Let's take the case of taking a shower early in the morning. If we do not have hot water, especially during winter, it is tapas to take an early morning shower. Taking a shower in the morning will help us to feel fresh and clean. That is why it is good to take a shower before our morning meditation and other spiritual practices. Unfortunately, due to our laziness and reluctance to get up early, our mind will give many reasons to avoid taking a shower.

Amma says that tapas can start with simple things like breaking the habit of drinking coffee, creating the habit of taking a morning shower or waiting to eat food only after chanting the 15th chapter of *Bhagavad Gita*. Tapas is a valuable tool we can use to tame our mind. Amma says that all of us have to practice some sort of tapas in our life, even in running a family. When a baby cries and you don't know the reason for the crying, it is a form of tapas to pacify the baby.

You must have heard of the Ayurvedic system of medicine. Along than the medicine itself, the discipline that we are supposed to follow after taking the medicine is also very important. Some food items have to be avoided if the Ayurvedic medicine is to have the intended effect. Sometimes we may not like the diet restrictions the doctor has prescribed for us, but if we want to benefit from the medicine, we have to follow the doctor's advice. In the same way, if we really want to get the full benefit of our spiritual practices, it is important to practice disciplines such as sacrifice, charity and penance.

THE VALUE OF PATIENCE

A few years ago a woman came to see Amma in Belgium. She had many physical problems and was crying while she was waiting in the darshan line. After darshan, Amma asked her to sit by Her side. I happened to be the one translating for Amma at that time. After some time, when the lady wanted to go home, she asked me to get some prasad from Amma. I asked Amma, but it was as though She didn't notice or even hear me. I asked Her a second time. But Amma didn't respond. Finally, mustering up more courage, I asked Amma a third time. "Amma, this lady wants some prasad from You." Amma asked me to keep quiet.

By then, this lady had become really impatient. She seemed agitated and said, "Swami, please give me the prasad. I have to go." But I didn't have the courage to ask Amma again. The lady waited for a few more minutes and then left without the prasad.

After about five minutes, Amma turned toward me and gave me the prasad (sacred ash) for that lady. I told Amma that she had already left. Amma said, "Oh... this would have solved her problems."

I felt very sorry because if she had waited for just five more minutes, her problems would have been solved. She was so impatient. In the presence of a Master like Amma, impatience and other negative attitudes can cost us dearly. Fortunately, the lady returned the next day for Devi Bhava. I immediately went up to her and told her, "You should not have left so soon. Just five minutes after you left, Amma gave me the prasad. The next time you come, try to be patient and spend more time with Amma." This time, she received the prasad from Amma. When I met this lady the following year, I learned that her health had improved.

After meeting Amma and being in Her presence, many of us get a taste of the calm and quiet state which it is possible for our mind to attain. This helps us to appreciate the value of Self-realization. Because we want to remain in this peaceful state, we are inspired to overcome our negative attitudes. Through developing good qualities like patience, tolerance and forbearance, the mind becomes calm and pure. This purity of mind will help us to have profound spiritual experiences and will ultimately prepare us for Self-realization.

WORSHIPPING THE GURU'S FEET

Just as the clouds obscure the sun, at present our Self is obscured by the ego and other negativities. But Amma can purify us. She is a purifier of hearts. When we offer our self, which is covered by the ego and attachments, it goes through the "Amma-purifier" and comes back to us as pure Self. Usually, when people prostrate to Amma, She touches their head and blesses them. This signifies that when we offer something with love and humility at Her lotus feet, it comes back to us as blessings. It's a perfect circle.

Many readers may wonder why we worship the Guru's feet. Some may ask, why don't we worship the head? Isn't the head the most important part of the body?

Worshipping the Guru's feet is symbolic of worshipping supreme knowledge and the Truth, because the Masters are established in Self-knowledge, the eternal Truth. Their feet represent the foundation on which they stand or the ground in which they are established. This foundation is *Atma Jnana* or Self-knowledge. Thus, when we prostrate at Amma's feet, we are symbolically worshipping Self-knowledge, the Truth that supports the whole creation.

When we stand before such great Masters, we become silent with awe and admiration. We feel we are totally insignificant. It is similar to standing in front of the great Himalayas. Seeing the height of those mountains, we are overwhelmed; we become silent and humble.

When we prostrate at the Master's feet, it represents our humility and surrender. The true spirit of humility and surrender can create the proper frame of mind to receive the grace and teachings of the Guru. In return, the Guru molds us into someone like Him or Her. That is the greatness of the Guru. In worldly life, no one wants a subordinate to become equal to him or her in status. But a Master is different. The Master wants all His or Her disciples to attain the same state of Self-realization that He or She experiences. This is because a Master's love is selfless. The Master's love isn't based on conditions or the qualifications of the disciple. There is nothing in the world to compare with this love.

GRATITUDE

As devotees, we are grateful to Amma. She has changed our lives dramatically. Her influence ranges from the way we greet our friends and our eating habits to the emotional and spiritual growth we are experiencing. Now, when we see each other, we don't say "Hi," or "Hello." We say, "Namah Shivaya." This form of salutation carries a significant meaning: "I bow down to the Auspicious One (within you)." Saying this helps us to behold one and the same God in every human being. In every aspect of our lives we feel Amma's presence and the changes Amma has created in us. We may or may not have changed our life-style, but our attitudes and perspective on life have changed a great deal. Above all, Amma has given us a glimpse into our own Self.

Though Amma doesn't expect us to feel grateful to Her, feeling gratitude toward Her will help us to attune to Her and remain open to Her grace and blessings. This gratitude means being conscious of every little act of kindness we receive from Amma as well as from the world.

When we feel sincere gratitude toward someone, the ego is in the process of diminishing. It is said that gratitude is the means of attracting the favor of God's mercy and forgiveness upon ourselves.

When we feel grateful toward somebody, there is no need to compare what we have done for that person with what he or she has done for us. Once you have done something good, forget about it. Remember only the good things done for you by others. The ego can creep in even while doing good things, so it is necessary to avoid keeping an account of what good we have done for others, and equally necessary not to forget what good we have received from others. The final goal of all our spiritual practices is to eliminate the ego.

I remember a story about a priest. One day, he had a special experience and was blessed with God's grace. That evening, as he was standing before the shrine, he prayed to God. "Oh Lord, I am deeply grateful to you. Your compassion and grace are so great. I am nothing. I am only an insignificant creature in Your presence."

As the priest was praying thus, the old caretaker over-heard his words. He also started praying aloud, "Oh Lord, I am nothing. I am an insignificant creature on whom You have showered Your compassion."

When the priest heard this, he became very annoyed. He thought, "Look who thinks he is also insignificant and nothing! He has the presumption to think he's just like me!"

The ego is very subtle. It will make us pretend we are the most egoless person in the world. What that priest felt was not gratitude; it was only a mask of his ego.

There is a story about a boy who fell into a river but didn't know how to swim. Though he struggled against the strong current and tried to make it back to the shore, he wasn't making much progress, and it seemed that he would drown. Seeing his plight, a man who was a strong swimmer leapt into the rushing waters and rescued the boy. When he was safe and sound on the shore, the boy expressed his sincere gratitude. "Thank you so much for saving my life," he said.

"You don't need to thank me," the man replied. "Just make sure that your life was worth saving."

Similarly, Amma doesn't want our thanks. Instead, let us express our gratitude toward Amma through our actions, words and thoughts. Only then can we repay Amma, at least to some extent, for what She is doing for us and what She has given us.

CHAPTER 16

THE SWEEPER OF THE WORLD

SWEEPING OUR MINDS

On August 29, 2000, as Amma left the United Nations General Assembly Hall after delivering Her major presentation at the Millennium World Peace Summit, She granted the media an opportunity to ask Her questions during a press conference. One of the reporters asked Her what She would do if She were chosen as the leader of the world. Amma said, "I do not want to be the world leader, but I would like to be a sweeper. I would like to sweep everybody's minds clean."

We may think that our minds are clean and Amma need only sweep the minds of other people, but only when we are faced with difficult circumstances do we get a glimpse of the real nature of our mind.

Amma tells a story about a very successful man. Along with money and fame, he had many enemies who were jealous of his success. One day as he went out for a walk, the neighbor's dog bit him. As it was a pet dog, he thought there was no danger of rabies, so he didn't seek any medical help. Some days later, he fell ill and went to the doctor. The doctor said, "It's too late for you. The dog that bit you was rabid, and your life is at risk." As soon as the man heard this, he immediately took his notepad out of his briefcase and began writing something down. Now the doctor felt apprehensive. He thought he shouldn't have told the man that his life was in danger. Instead, he should have tried to console him. The doctor thought, "He is probably writing his will." In order to cheer up his patient, the doctor said, "Don't worry, we have some of the latest medicine. I will try to save your life. Never lose hope. There's no need for you to write your will right now."

The man looked up at the doctor and said, "Doctor, I am not such a fool that I would write my will. You know that when you are bitten by a rabid dog, you can be a carrier of that deadly disease."

"Yes. So what?" said the doctor.

The man continued, "I am making a list of the people I want to bite!"

If we are perfectly pure, then Amma won't need to sweep our minds clean, but most of us need Her humble service.

THE MASTER FORESEES THE FUTURE

When I came to the ashram for the first time, I had my own plans for my future: holding a high profile job, marrying a rich, beautiful girl, building a big house, etc. During one Devi Bhava in those early days, Amma pointed to me and said to another devotee, "Go and sit next to that brahmachari." I was surprised to hear Amma speaking of me as a brahmachari as I had not even dreamt of becoming a brahmachari. I thought Amma was not, after all, as all-knowing as people made Her out to be. I thought Amma was going to be miserably wrong in Her prediction.

Then after three years, the bank where I worked granted my request to be transferred to my hometown. Actually, the reason I had come to see Amma in the first place was to get Her blessing for a quick transfer to my hometown. Having received the transfer, I realized that what Amma had said about my becoming a brahmachari would also probably come true.

After the transfer, every day at the bank seemed like years to me. I felt I could not work there. I couldn't concentrate and made many mistakes in my accounting. My superiors wondered what was wrong with me. I felt a huge void in my life. Only now that I was away from Amma did I realize the power of Her unconditional love. I thought I'd become a psychological wreck if I didn't get to see Amma immediately. So I left the bank and my hometown and rushed to the ashram without even telling my superiors or submitting a leave of absence letter.

Amma instructed me to return to my job and get a transfer to a branch of the bank near Amma's ashram. It was to be a few more years before Amma would permit me to resign from my job.

Finally, I came back to the ashram again after getting a transfer to a small town near the ashram, called Karunagappally. While I had been working in my hometown, my parents thought that I had come to my senses and would soon forget, once and for all, about the ashram and Amma. When I applied for a transfer and came back to the ashram, they were shocked and upset. Once again they started looking for ways to bring me back home.

My maternal grandfather came to see me and tempted me, saying that if I returned home he would buy me a brand new car and a nice house. Somehow I managed to send him back, saying I was grateful to him for his generous offer and would think deeply about it.

After a few months I received a letter from home saying that my mother was seriously ill in the hospital and that I had to come home immediately. When I read that letter, I was worried. So I took the letter to Amma and translated the contents. Amma listened patiently but didn't say anything. I was getting restless, wanting Her to give me a definite answer. After some time I again reminded Amma about the letter. In a slightly annoyed tone, She asked me to keep quiet. I became even more restless and agitated. I even thought that Amma must have some selfish intention, which was why She was neither giving me an answer nor letting me go home.

I didn't understand then that when the Master doesn't answer a question, the disciple should just drop it without making a big fuss about it. I decided to ask Amma again the next day. When I asked Her for an answer about the letter, She became very serious and said, "Ramakrishna, I want to tell you the truth, whether you like it or not. I have nothing to gain by keeping you here in the ashram. Whether you stay or not doesn't make any difference to me.

"First, I do not think your mother is as sick as you think. She is definitely sad that you are staying in the ashram. Everything will be all right. But if you go home, you might never come back here. Also, if you go home now, you are spoiling the chances of your parents coming to spirituality. You can decide what you want to do. I am just telling you the consequences."

This is the beauty of the Masters. They will not force us to do anything. They are full of love. Love cannot force; nor can love be violent. Love can only be soft and gentle. In the *Bhagavad Gita*, Lord Krishna gives the whole *Gita* of over 700 verses to Arjuna in the battlefield. After explaining and answering all of Arjuna's questions and clearing his doubts, Krishna says to Arjuna, "I have told you what I have to tell you. Now you can do as you like." *("Yadecchasi tadha kuru.")*

Having heard Amma's reply, I decided not to go home, as I wanted neither to be away from Amma, nor to be the cause of my parents not coming to the spiritual path. As Amma had predicted, everything became all right at home. There was no serious problem with my mother's health. However, my parents became even more upset and angry because it appeared to them that I didn't choose to come home even though I had been told that my mother was seriously ill.

Eventually, they lodged a complaint with the police, saying that I was having mental problems and that the ashram was keeping me there by force and exploiting me. Police officials were sent to inquire about the complaint.

Seeing a team of police arrive at the ashram, the villagers gathered around hoping for some hot, sensational news. I soon discovered that the police had come to the ashram looking for me. The chief police officer asked me a few questions and finally asked me to come to the police station the next day.

At the police station, an inquiry was conducted in the presence of my father. I answered all of the police officer's questions to his satisfaction and convinced him that I was staying in the ashram out of my own free will and not because of anyone's coercion or force. Finally, he closed the complaint file, told my father that I was fine, and explained that the police could not force me to leave the ashram.

I came back to the ashram and explained everything to Amma. I felt sorry for my father, but I was also angry with him for creating a scene at the ashram by bringing the police. The villagers had already started spreading some rumors about the police visiting the ashram. I asked Amma to make sure that my father would not repeat this in the future. But Amma expressed only love for my parents. She wasn't at all upset with them. She asked me not to be angry with my parents. She told me that my father would one day come to the ashram, become a devotee and breathe his last breath with the divine names on his lips.

Once again, I doubted Amma's words. I couldn't imagine my father coming to the ashram, let alone becoming a devotee, because he and my mother were so angry with Amma.

After a couple of years, my father, with a few other relatives, came to the bank where I was working and made me write another transfer request to the bank authorities so that I would be transferred back to my native town. Since I didn't want to create a scene at the bank when so many customers were present, I just signed the letter thinking that once my father left the place I could cancel my transfer request. Accordingly, that evening I submitted another letter requesting that the earlier application be considered cancelled.

I came back to the ashram and told Amma what had happened at the bank. Amma was doubtful whether the authorities would consider my second letter (the request letter to cancel my transfer request). So Amma advised me to give one more letter to make sure that my request for transfer would be cancelled. I told Amma that it wouldn't be necessary as I had already given such a letter. I didn't want to keep giving letter after letter. However, soon I paid the price for taking Amma's words lightly and for not doing what She had instructed. Within a few months, my transfer order came, and I was ordered to join the new branch, effective immediately. Somehow my father had been able to obtain a quick transfer order for me. Later Amma told me that my letter requesting the cancellation of my transfer request had not reached the authorities, and that this was why She had wanted me to send one more letter.

I was once again upset and angry with my father, but Amma said that it made no sense to get angry with my father because it was my own fault. I had to admit my mistake, but I reminded Amma that my father had not yet come to the ashram and become Her devotee as She had predicted some years back. If he had, then this problem would not have happened. Amma said that he would definitely come to the ashram, and that I should be patient.

I wanted to resign from the bank immediately as I didn't want to go to the new branch. Amma insisted that I take a long leave of absence instead of resigning. Only after some time did She allow me to resign. Finally, the problem of the transfer came to an end once and for all.

One day, to my surprise, almost eight years after Amma had said that my father would come to the ashram, he came to see Amma. After his first darshan with Amma, he changed completely. He started visiting the ashram frequently and took mantra initiation from Amma. Thus, what Amma had said about him came true.

Regarding a Mahatma knowing the truth about the future, Amma says, "What a Mahatma says may or may not be true at the moment it is spoken, but it will become true because Mahatmas are established in Truth." Not only do Mahatmas speak the truth, truth follows their words.

One day my father came to the ashram to get Amma's blessings during Devi Bhava. After his darshan, he came away from the stage and sat in the hall chanting Amma's 108 Names. As he was leaving the temple, he felt dizzy and sat down again. He asked for water, drank it, and in a few minutes breathed his last without any difficulty. The devotee who gave him water later told me that my father was chanting Amma's name. He was also holding Amma's prasad in his hands. Thus, what Amma said about him came true to the very letter. Later Amma confirmed that he had been chanting Amma's mantra when he died. She said that he wouldn't have to be born again. He had merged with Her. Even though I was sad when I heard about his death, I felt happy that he died chanting Amma's name and that he would not have to be born again.

After a few years my mother also came to the ashram, and now she is one of the residents of the ashram. She says that she is very happy to be with Amma and she doesn't need to bother about her children, grandchildren and other family members as all of them have become devotees of Amma. She knows that Amma will take care of them.

ASHRAM LIFE

It is commonly held that it is not proper to take to a spiritual path while you are young. People usually think that spiritual life or ashram life should be adopted only after retirement or at a later stage of one's life. This concept is incorrect. The scriptures say that if you have dispassion toward worldly life and feel a spiritual inclination, you can take to the spiritual path even at a young age. More than the age of a person, what matters is the disinterest in worldly things and achievements and earnest desire to know the Truth. After retirement, a person may not be physically able to adapt to a spiritual way of life—at that age it might be too difficult to sit in a proper posture in order to meditate or to find the energy to serve others.

When young men and women decide to join Amma's ashram in India, they sometimes experience opposition from their families. Families are generally much more close-knit in India than they are in the West. While young people in western countries often move away from home by the age of eighteen, children in India usually live with their parents until they are married. It is not uncommon to see a forty-year-old unmarried person living at home. Even after they get married, many couples continue to live with the husband's parents.

One of the main reasons my parents didn't want me to join the ashram, apart from their love and attachment to me, was that I was the eldest son. Usually, in the Indian tradition, it is the eldest son who shares the responsibility of the family with the father. When the father or mother dies, it is usually the eldest son who performs the funeral rites and the regular ancestral rites. Moreover, I had two sisters yet to be married. My parents were worried that no one would come forward to marry them if they knew that the eldest son had become a monk. Of course, many people respect monks, but they may not want anyone from their family to become a monk. Many people think that if a person becomes a monk at a young age that there must be something wrong with such a person or with that family.

Suppose someone gets married. He or she may take care of a family of four or five. But if a person joins the ashram, he or she can serve a much wider circle of people.

Amma gives the example of a coconut. If we use a coconut for cooking, it may be enough for a few people. If, instead, that coconut is used to grow a coconut tree, we will get many coconuts, which will be useful for many more people. Additional coconut trees can also be grown from those coconuts, yielding an even larger crop.

When men and women join the ashram to become brahmacharis or brahmacharinis, their love becomes expansive. Amma's living example inspires them to become more and more selfless. Staying in an ashram, especially with a great Master like Amma, definitely has a positive effect; people who do so become disciplined and cultivate many good qualities. If parents are really interested in the happiness and the character of their children, there is no reason why they should discourage them from joining Amma's ashram. The ashram is not teaching anything harmful. In fact, many who come are transformed and begin leading a righteous life when they otherwise might not have done so. In this way, many people who might otherwise have been a problem to their parents and to society, are put on the right track by Amma.

In my case, because I stayed in the ashram rather than returning to my home and family, my parents came to see Amma. As a result of meeting Amma, they certainly benefited greatly even though they initially felt sad and upset. They would not have received these benefits had I gone back home and stayed with them.

Many people ask the brahmacharis whether it is right to go and stay in the ashram without taking care of their parents. Amma tells the brahmacharis, "If there is no one to take care of your parents, the ashram can take good care of them. Bring them here." Even if adult children stay with their parents, how many take proper care of their parents as they get older—especially once the children are married? Also, many adult children in India go abroad to take a job. They may visit their parents only once in a few years, but their parents do not find anything wrong with that.

Amma knows that the parents, because of their attachment to their children and the expectations they have of them, do not always see the logic in their children joining the ashram. They do not understand the potential benefits not only to their children, but to society at large. Some may say that by joining the ashram, young men and women are not adhering to their dharma toward their family and society. But such people overlook the fact that spiritual aspirants also have their dharma, and that sometimes this dharma is higher or more important than another dharma, leading as it does to a life of service and spiritual practice which will ultimately benefit the world.

Suppose a person is in the army and suddenly a war breaks out. However loving he may be toward his wife and children, he will have to go away from them and fight in the war because that is his dharma. He may even have to give up his life if the situation demands it. In such a situation his duty toward his country is more important than his duties toward his family. Thus, depending on the situation, one dharma becomes more important than another.

Of course, spiritual life is not for brahmacharis and brahmacharinis alone. There are also many householders living at Amritapuri. Husbands, wives and children are dedicating their lives to spiritual practice and service to the world. There are also many who are unable to live at the ashram full-time but spend as much time there as they can. And there are Amma's devotees all over the world, serving Amma in their communities through the ashrams, centers, and satsang groups, trying to convert their every action into worship of Amma. Through financial contributions and hard work, Amma's householder children help support the ashram and many of Her charitable activities. Amma says that sometimes it is Her householder children, immersed in worldly responsibilities and unable to spend much time with Her physically, who are truly enjoying Her presence within, as their hearts are full of longing and their minds are always dwelling on Her.

Whether a person is a brahmachari or a householder, as long as one has sincere longing to reach the goal and a Satguru like Amma as a guide, Self-realization can be attained. In fact, many of the ancient saints and sages were householders. It is up to each one of us, wherever we are and whatever we are doing, to walk forward along the razor's edge.

A BLESSED OPPORTUNITY

"I want my life to be like an incense stick
which burns itself out giving fragrance to the world.
I want to breathe my last wiping somebody's tears
and consoling them on my shoulder." — Amma

Amma is living Her entire life, day and night, for the sake of Her children. She always wants to spend Her time with us and for us. During my 25 years of association with Amma, I can count on my fingers the number of days She has not given darshan. She travels all over the world and yet never takes a vacation and never has the luxury of sightseeing or entertainment.

Amma sleeps at the most one or two hours a night no matter where She is in the world. She often doesn't sleep at all. Whenever She is not giving darshan, She is attending to the needs of Her ever-growing network of charities and other institutions, meeting with government officials and other dignitaries who seek Her audience, leading Her children in singing bhajans every evening, and advising the more than 2,000 ashram residents on their spiritual progress and personal problems. Even after all that, Her day is not over. Each night She spends hour upon hour reading letters from Her devotees. When a newspaper reporter in New York City asked Amma about the secret of not getting tired even after giving darshan to devotees for hours and hours, Amma said, "I am connected to the eternal source of energy and not to a battery which loses its energy every time it is used."

Amma says that She wants to ease the pain and suffering of everyone in the world. But, as it will not be physically possible for Her to help and console every person on the planet, She wants each of us to become Her hands, reaching out to those in need. Actually, Amma wants each of Her children to become another Amma, spreading the light of unconditional love and compassion throughout the world. She says that She wants us to grow to such an extent that even the wind that touches our body will be beneficial to others. Every moment of Her life is dedicated to this goal.

As Amma's children, we are blessed to be contemporaries of Amma and to have faith in Her. It is our responsibility and our joy to make that faith stronger in every way possible. Refer back constantly to the series of positive experiences you and others have had with Amma to reinforce your faith in Her. Each experience carries with it a different message for our life.

Amma's simplicity and humility camouflage Her greatness. Her untainted love makes us feel so comfortable and so familiar that we take Her to be an ordinary person. Once in a while, like a bolt of a lightning, we recall Her greatness. At other times we have to contemplate and meditate on Her divinity. Otherwise, Her motherly love and the care and concern that She shows can easily carry us away. We need this love and affection for our spiritual growth, but if it carries us away, there is a chance that we might miss Her greatness, just like Arjuna who for a long time took Lord Krishna to be simply his friend. To worldly eyes, Amma seems to be nothing more than a loving human being. Amma uses this appearance to conceal Her greatness. Even though Amma acts as if She is unaware of many things, She knows everything. Amma has proven this on many occasions. In truth, She is the incarnation of Parashakti, the Supreme Power—the Divine Mother of the Universe.

Let us try to make full use of this magnificent opportunity. Whether or not we attain the goal of Self-realization in this lifetime, the spiritual progress we make will stay with us. If, by chance, we do not reach the goal in this life, we can start from where we left off in our next life—we don't have to start all over again. So let us remember Amma with love and longing, and persist in our spiritual practices with patience, enthusiasm, and optimistic faith. In this way, whether we are physically close to Her or far away, we can always feel Amma's presence and finally merge in Her lotus feet.

Om Amriteswaryai Namah

GLOSSARY

adharma – Unrighteousness. The opposite of dharma

adhi bhautikam – Disturbances we experience from the world around us

adhi daivikam – Disturbances that come from natural forces

adhyatmikam – Disturbances that come from within

Advaita – The philosophy of non-duality

ahamkara – Ego or "the sense of an existence separate from the rest of the universe"

Arjuna – The third of the five Pandava brothers. A great archer who is one of the heroes of the *Mahabharata*. It is Arjuna whom Krishna addresses in the *Bhagavad Gita*.

arrta – People who are suffering

artharthi – People who seek riches or seek to fulfill their desires

asana – Hatha yoga posture

Atman – The Self or Consciousness

Atma jnana – Knowledge of the Self

AUM – Also "Om." According to the Vedic scriptures, this is the primordial sound in the universe. All other sounds arise out of Om and resolve back into Om

avadhut – A saint whose behavior does not conform with social norms

Ayurveda – The ancient traditional Indian system of medicine

Bhagavad Gita – "Song of the Lord." Bhagavad = of the Lord; gita = song. The teachings Lord Krishna gave Arjuna on the Kurukshetra battlefield at the beginning of the Mahabharata War. It is a practical guide for daily life and contains the essence of Vedic wisdom

Bhagavatam – A book describing the lives of the ten Incarnations of Lord Vishnu, especially Krishna and his childhood antics. It upholds the supremacy of devotion as a path to union with God

bhajan – Devotional song

bhakti – Spiritual devotion and love

bhava – Divine mood or attitude (see Devi Bhava)

bhiksha – Alms

Bhishma – Grandfather of the Pandavas and Kauravas. Though he fought on the side of the Kauravas during the Mahabharata War, he was a champion of dharma, and was sympathetic to the victorious Pandavas. After Krishna, he is the most important character in the *Mahabharata*

bhoga – Enjoyment of sense pleasures

brahmachari – A celibate male disciple who practices spiritual disciplines and is usually being trained by a spiritual master. Brahmacharini is the female equivalent

Brahmasthanam Temple – Born out of Amma's divine intuition, these unique temples are the first to show multiple deities on a single icon. The icon is four-sided, displaying Ganesha, Shiva, Devi and Rahu, emphasizing the inherent unity underlying the manifold aspects of the Divine. There are sixteen such temples throughout India and one in Mauritius

Brindavan – The childhood home of Lord Krishna, where much of his *lila* (divine play) unfolded

chapatti – Flat, round bread, similar to a tortilla

danam - Charity

darshan – An audience with or a vision of the Divine or of a holy person

Deepavali – "Festival of Lights," also called Diwali. Primarily celebrates Rama's homecoming to Ayodhya after fourteen years in exile, but has other associations as well. In some parts of India, it is in celebration of Lakshmi, Saraswati and Durga. Signifies the victory of light over darkness

Devi – Goddess. The Divine Mother

Devi Bhava – "The Divine Mood of Devi." The state in which Amma reveals Her oneness and identity with the Divine Mother

dharma – In Sanskrit, dharma means "that which upholds (Creation)." Most commonly it is used to indicate that which is responsible for the harmony of the universe. Other meanings include: righteousness, duty, responsibility

gopi – The gopis were cowherd girls and milkmaids who lived in Brindavan. They were Krishna's closest devotees, and were known for their supreme devotion to the Lord. They exemplify the most intense love for God

Guha – The boatman who ferried Rama across the Ganges

Haridwar – Sacred pilgrimage town in the foothills of the Himalayas

Janaka – King in ancient India, renowned for being Self-realized yet never neglecting his worldly duty of governing the kingdom

japa – Repetition of a mantra

jijnasu – Person who is sincerely interested in knowledge, especially that of the Truth, or God

jnana danam – Giving knowledge as charity

jnani – A person who has realized God or the Self. One who knows the Truth

Kalari – The small temple where Amma used to hold Krishna and Devi Bhava darshan in the early days of the ashram and where daily pujas are still conducted

karma – Action or deed. Also the chain of effects which our actions produce

Karna – King from the *Mahabharata* who is considered to be one of the most charitable people in history

Katha Upanishad – One of the principle Upanishads, in which a young boy travels to meet Yama, the Lord of Death. Yama answers the boy's questions about the Self

Kauravas – The 100 children of Dhritharasthra and Gandhari, of whom the unrighteous Duryodhana was the eldest. The Kauravas were the enemies of their cousins, the virtuous Pandavas, whom they fought in the Mahabharata War

Krishna – The principle incarnation of Vishnu. He was born into a royal family but grew up with foster parents and lived as a young cowherd in Brindavan where He was loved and worshipped by his devoted companions, the gopis and gopas (the cowherd boys and girls). Krishna later became the ruler of Dwaraka. He was a friend and advisor to His cousins, the Pandavas, especially Arjuna, to whom He served as charioteer during the Mahabharata War, and to whom He revealed His teachings as the *Bhagavad Gita*

lila – divine play

Mahabharata – One of the two great Indian historical epics, the other being the *Ramayana*. It is a great treatise on dharma and spirituality. The story deals mainly with the conflict between the Pandavas and Kauravas and the great war at Kurukshetra. Containing 100,000 verses, it is the longest epic poem in the world, written about 3,200 B.C. by the sage Vyasa

maitri – Friendliness toward all beings

mamakara – Possessive attachment. The sense of owner-ship or "mine-ness"

Mata Amritanandamayi Devi – Amma's official monas-tic name, meaning Mother of Immortal Bliss

moksha – Final spiritual liberation

mon – Malayalam for "son." Amma will often whisper this into the ears of Her male children while giving darshan. *Mol* means "daughter"

Mount Kailas – Situated in the Himalayas, Mount Kailas is one of the most sacred pilgrimage sites. Traditionally referred to as the abode of Shiva by some Hindu scriptures

mudra – Physical gesture with spiritual significance, often expressed with the hands

Namadev – An ardent devotee of the Lord who reached the great heights of God-realization

Om Amriteswaryai Namah – Mantra sacred to Amma's devotees, meaning, "Salutations to the Goddess of Immortality (Amma)"

Om Namah Shivaya – Powerful mantra meaning "I bow down to the Eternally Auspicious One"

Pandavas – The five brothers – Yudhisthira, Bhima, Arjuna, Nakula and Sahadeva – who were the sons of King Pandu and the heroes of the epic *Mahabharata*

pappadam – Thin, round and flat crispy bread

paramartika satta – The absolute reality

Parashakti – The Supreme Power

Parvati – Consort of Lord Shiva

Patanjali – Ancient Indian sage, best known for his famous Yoga Sutras

prarabdha – The fruits of actions from previous lives that one is destined to experience in this present life

prasad – Blessed offering or gift from a holy person or temple, often in the form of food

pratabhasika satta – Apparent reality

puja – Ritualistic or ceremonial worship

Rama – The divine hero of the epic *Ramayana*. An incarnation of Lord Vishnu, He is considered to be the ideal of dharma and virtue

rishi – Self-realized seers or sages who experienced the Supreme Truth, and expressed this insight through the composition of the oldest and most sacred Indian texts, the Vedas

sadhana – Spiritual practice

samadhi – Oneness with God. A transcendental state in which one loses all sense of individual identity

Sanatana Dharma – "The Eternal Way of Life." The original and traditional name for Hinduism

sankalpa – Divine resolve

sannyasi – A monk who has taken formal vows of renunciation (sannyasa). A sannyasi traditionally wears an ochre-colored cloth representing the burning away of all desires. The female equivalent is a sannyasini

Satguru – A Self-realized spiritual master

satsang – Sat = truth, being; sanga = association with. Being in the company of the Mahatmas; also listening to a spiritual talk or discussion

seva – Selfless service that is dedicated to God

shanti – Peace

Sita – Rama's holy consort. In India she is considered to be the ideal of womanhood

Srimad Bhagavatam – See *Bhagavatam*. Srimad means "auspicious"

Sudama – Pious Brahmin and childhood friend of Krishna

Sudhamani – Amma's given name, meaning "Pure Jewel"

tabla – Small Indian drum

tantra – A system of worship to gain the blessings of a higher power. Emphasis is placed on *mudras* rather than mantras

tapas – Austerities, penance

Tiruvannamallai – Town at the foot of the sacred Arunachala hill in the South Indian state of Tamil Nadu, where the famous saint Ramana Maharshi lived

Tulsidas – Indian poet and saint, well-known for his composition of the *Ramayana* in Hindi

udarah – Noble

Upanishad – The concluding portions of the Vedas dealing with the philosophy of Non-dualism

vasana – Latent tendencies or subtle desires within the mind which manifest as action and habits

Vedic – Of or pertaining to the ancient Vedas

vyavaharika satta – Relative reality

yagna – Worship without expectation of personal gain

Yagnavalkya – A great sage who figures as a principal teacher in the Vedas and Upanishads. He was the Guru to King Janaka

Yashoda – Foster mother to Krishna

yoga – "To unite." Union with the Supreme Being. A broad term, it also refers to the various practical methods through which one can attain oneness with the Divine. A path that leads to Self-realization

Yogi – One who has attained the ultimate state of Yoga.

INDEX TO STORIES